# Mindful
# LIVING

MW00390704

# Mindful
# LIVING

*Everyday practices for a
sacred and happy life*

## Katie Manitsas

**ROCKPOOL**
PUBLISHING

A Rockpool book
PO Box 252
Summer Hill, NSW 2130
www.rockpoolpublishing.com.au

First published in 2019
Copyright text © Katie Manitsas, 2019

All rights reserved. No part of this publication may be reproduced, stored in a retrieval system,
or transmitted in any form or by any means, electronic, mechanical, photocopying, recording
or otherwise, without the prior written permission of the publisher.

ISBN 978-1-925682-85-4

A catalogue record for this book is available from the
National Library of Australia.

Cover design by Farrah Careem
Editing by Lisa Macken
Images supplied by Valerita Valerosa
Typesetting and internal design by Sonya Murphy
Printed and bound in China
10 9 8 7 6 5 4 3 2 1

'You have learnt the art of spiritual love – so share it clearly for the benefit of others. You can't wait for the opportunity to come to you. You have to make it happen. If you have the desire to do some service for Krishna, nothing can stop you. That's between you and Krishna; you and your spiritual master.

If you just take one step, Krishna takes ten steps towards you. You just have to start it. The whole world is suffering so if we can help them we should not hold back. The chance is given for everyone to become a great devotee; an advocate for love supreme.'

– *Narayani Dasi*

# Contents

# Dedication

Thank you to my teachers in all forms: my family, my friends and community, and my teachers of many years – Sharon Gannon, David Life, Maya Tiwari and Simon Low. Gratitude also to Radhanath Swami and the ISKCON community in Sydney (especially Madhuri Devi Dasi) and in Murwillumbah Lila Kirtana. You all had an important influence on me during the writing of this book and I am so grateful.

Guru Brahma, Guru Vishnu, Guru devo Maheshwara, Guru Sakshat, param Brahma, tasmai shri guravay namah.

I bow down in reverence to all my teachers. The teacher that is this life I have been given and continue to live. The teacher that is all difficulty and hardship on my path. The teacher who is nearby, and the teacher who is beyond all this, loving and supreme.

My gratitude to the Wise Earth School of Ayurveda for permitting me to relay some of its core education principles and practices based in the ancient tenets of sadhana and ahimsa in this book. My gratitude to Maya Tiwari, the founder of Wise Earth Ayurveda teachings, for restoring and reintroducing Inner Medicine Healing practices of sadhana into modern-day Ayurveda education. This work has a critical impact on the need for inner harmony, peace and healing in our world. Wise Earth Ayurveda education has also helped me to find balance and harmony in my everyday life and purpose.

# Introduction

Within these pages you will find reference to many ancient scriptures, from yoga traditions and beyond. All scripture is there to offer wisdom teachings and to uplift. Often a wide range of characters are used to tell stories, of sinners and saints, of family and circumstances that can be used for spiritual teaching. Scripture allows us to engage with something very old, which can be reassuring for modern people. The fact that the teachings of yoga are so old is also reassuring – so many things come and go, yet these practices have not become obsolete; they are still useful. Yoga's ancient lineage gives us a feeling of being called back to something that doesn't change amid the transient nature of daily life. Many of these scriptures refer to the idea of 'God', an idea that for many has very strong and culturally specific associations. In yoga philosophy 'God' is a broad term that can mean something like the 'higher' or more spiritual part of yourself, as well as the powers of goodness, joy and potential both within each of us and around us. I invite you to think about God in the broadest and most accessible terms possible as you ponder the ancient yogic teachings and not to get too caught up in a one-dimensional image or idea of who or what God is.

A main theme of this book is devotion, or what is referred to in the ancient Indian language of Sanskrit as *bhakti*. In Patanjali's Yoga Sutras, the ancient text that holds the foundation for the philosophical teachings of yoga, we find two sutras or threads that have helped me to embody and live these devotional (bhakti) teachings rather than just think about them abstractly.

'By giving your life and identity to God you attain the identity of God.' – *Yoga Sutra translation: Sharon Gannon, Chapter 1, sutra 23*

This sutra speaks to the importance of a non-intellectual approach. Another way of thinking about it is in the Christian teaching of 'not my will but thy will be done'. For many of us in modern culture this can be a tough teaching to dive into, we are taught from a very young age to be autonomous and self-directing. Our ideas about self-worth and self-esteem are confusingly tangled up in ideas of not subjugating ourselves to another. We mistake being humble for being suppressed or dominated in a negative way. In my own experience the opposite is true; I have found there is enormous liberation in becoming less self-directing and in asking for help and guidance from a higher power. The name of that higher power is not important. Whether that is God, Krishna, or simply a wise universal consciousness, realising that my will and my self-direction is often muddied and confused by all kinds of conflicting ideas and emotions has helped me. I can step aside from what Patanjali calls 'chitta vritti' (mental chatter) and instead drop into something deeper – Divine will. In this way, I feel myself moving closer to God and to a truly nourishing way of being in the world that is of service to others and to myself. It is a less whimsical and more steady way of approaching life's challenges.

Ultimately, because I also do believe that God's love is inside me anyway, what I'm really bowing down to or giving my life and identity to is the highest part of myself. I am bowing to my fullest spiritual potential rather than my emotions and feelings, which years of meditation have shown me clearly are transient, irrational and always changing. Attaining the identity of God means, in part at least, anchoring into something deeper and steadier than the daily chatter of my distracted mind.

The second sutra that has helped me put bhakti into action in my own life is:

'Concentration on the Divine produces lightness and self-confidence.' – *Yoga Sutra translation: Sharon Gannon, Chapter 1, sutra 36*

The self-confidence Master Patanjali speaks of here is powerful. It is nothing less than the sense that you are meant to be here, on this planet, at this time, in human form, for a sacred task. That might sound obvious, but it is a truth that many of us struggle to embrace. We feel we are not entitled to the abundance we have and we struggle to shine as brightly as we know we can. All the thoughts and behaviours we have that keep us trapped in poor body image, low self-esteem, dysfunctional relationships, toxic jobs, material addictions stem from a lack of self-confidence. If we really knew our worth and our power we wouldn't waste so much time in that wallowing. Instead we would focus sharply on what our *dharma*, or true calling, is in this lifetime. We would polish and sharpen the skills and gifts we have been given and offer them out in loving service. We would be the best we can be and do the best we can do, finding a path we are drawn to for that calling.

Patanjali even reminds us that this wouldn't be a heavy or arduous task. It won't feel overwhelming or sanctimonious when your dharma starts calling you and you begin to resonate with it. It will be light! Easeful! You will be filled with a sense of being in the right place at the right time, and synchronicities will start to unfold. This is the promise for those of us who concentrate on the Divine rather than concentrating on Facebook or shopping or the faults we perceive in others.

I've been writing for as long as I can remember; certainly endless notebooks and journals were filled as a teenager. Some of my early writing reflected my interest in the Bible as the first spiritual text I was given access to. Later I began to craft my own simple poems and other worlds opened up to me through reading and listening. The Celtic festivals marking the long days of the summer solstice, the harvest in autumn and the moving into stillness of the winter solstice all sang to me through the months and years of my youth in England and through the pages of books I devoured in order to understand more deeply the spirit of the place and time into which I was born. As I write this I am soon to turn 40, and when I was a young adult the internet didn't exist. I am surprisingly grateful for this, as it meant that knowledge was acquired more slowly and was more sacred. I was grateful for the wisdom I was exposed to, particularly for the wise women who supported my spiritual growth, because they were way-showers and knowledge bearers without whom I would not have grown in the ways I did.

I've had the great fortune to always be held and supported by a wonderful tribe of women. Throughout my whole life I've had not only friends but elders to turn to and ask for help when needed. I feel now, as I begin to age, the calling of moving a little closer to the role of elder myself, a pull that is stronger year by year as I observe my young children growing up. Author Lisa Lister describes wise women in generations past as 'keepers of arcane, sacred knowledge. They had many skills including the sacred observation of seasonal customs, healing and understanding and recognising the roots of the future in the past and present. They also held sacred the spiritual lives of the communities they served. This knowledge was stored and kept safe, with most of it being passed down orally through words and song, committed to memory rather than books.'

Yoga is to 'yoke with the Divine', to move closer to God. There are so many ways to do that, and it has worked for me to have cultivated my own personal relationship with the Divine through several strands of practice and influence. I know some do not agree with this but in my experience getting closer to God is not about how much knowledge we have access to but rather how applied that knowing is. It is about true remembering based on our ancestry, a memory that is visceral and alive with prana, not dry and academic. That is why I have written this book about sadhana. *Sadhana* means to act, to do something, to be in the world yet deeply connected to Spirit. I have long felt that my dharma in this lifetime is deeply connected to service (and having four children has tested this in the most hands-on way imaginable!), and I now begin to understand that service as 'holding sacred the spiritual lives of the communities I serve' – starting with my immediate circle of friends and family, and the yoga students I am so fortunate to teach.

'It makes our minds feel bright and clear when we hear someone say that our real purpose in life is to help and serve others.'
– *Geshe Michael Roache*

In these pages we will focus deeply on yoga practices and philosophy (and there is much magic inherent there – enough for many, many lifetimes of practice), as well as activism and the rhythm of the seasons according to ayurveda. I will encourage you to animate more deeply your intuition, to light candles and create altars not just as a remembrance of sacred space but as an awakening of magic and mystery. In growth and transformation, we come to expect the unexpected and intuition starts to strengthen as a tool we can use in our lives. There is a depth of emotion before consciousness arises or insight unfolds; dreams, impulses and wild creative bursts abound. As my teacher, the co-founder of Jivamukti Yoga Sharon Gannon, says, 'magic is a shift in perception'. As I'm writing these words I feel they are coming from this magical kind of a place, and I hope they will hold some power for transformation in your own life as you read them.

As we explore sadhana, or spiritual practices, a strong focus on bhakti (devotion) and mantra (chanting) will be with us for the journey. Sadhana is such a broad path and might include learning about herbal medicine and energy medicine from flowers and plants or practising ritual and sacred observation. There is sadhana in remembering and knowing that what we do, say and think today matters because the roots of the future are already present in this moment. This has become reflected in my yoga teaching and teaching in general, which is slowly morphing to include more and more circle work, ritual, intuition and the creation of sacred space. It may serve you to sometimes allow yourself to let go of familiar methods and frameworks (where you might worry you are 'doing things wrong') and open more to spacious creative expression.

I do acknowledge, however, that through familiar methods, particularly the Jivamukti Yoga method, the intuition and self-awareness in me developed to this place of creative expression. As a younger woman I needed methods and frameworks more. Perhaps that true self-confidence that Patanjali speaks of was still a glowing ember. As I move into middle age, it's a roaring fire. I still love the boundaries and discipline of methodical frameworks and without them I would be lost, at sea in a world of too many possibilities, but I also now see and crave the need for trusting my own flow and wisdom as well as that given to me from my teachers. I hope in this book, which is an offering to you, you feel a little of that wisdom and more importantly a permission to follow and awaken your own inner wisdom.

Please do not mistake a fluidity of methodologies and schools of thought with a lack of reverence for my teachers and the work they have shared with me. These teachings have saved me and served me for decades now, and it is in humble gratitude and deep pranam that I thank my teachers for their tireless work and creative spirits. I hope I do them justice in what I have to offer, and I hope as our journeys unfold – each one of us – that we find our own brave and powerful paths. I hope we are informed by our teachers and the methods we have diligently applied in our lives but enlivened by the self-confidence of our own heart's calling. His Divine Grace A.C. Bhaktivedanta Swami Prabhupada (known as Srila Prabhupada), the enlightened swami who founded the International Society of Krishna Consciousness (ISKCON), suggests that our dharma – our calling in life – is the service we offer that we know in our hearts sustains our existence. It is what we feel is of absolute value to us and for us to offer out. For me, the work I do and also writing about it is part of my service, and I feel honoured to be blessed with the clarity of knowing this and having the opportunity to do so.

Some of the teachings you will find in this book will not be new to you, but it is my goal to view as ongoing the role of the student in spiritual life. My level of knowledge is not fixed, and you never know what you may learn even in hearing the same teachings offered again and again. In the application of knowledge there is a second lesson. First we understand something intellectually, then we apply that understanding. You have to use spiritual knowledge in order for it to be effective, through invoking the desire to learn something. In asking for support to retain what we have learned, the teachings start to stick.

# CHAPTER I

# Steady foundations

*The practices of non-violence and devotion*
*as a foundation for spiritual life*

'Be silent and count your blessings, endless Grace has come.' – *Rumi*

## The practices of sadhana and ahimsa

Wise Earth Ayurveda describes sadhana as 'remembering and knowing what we do, say and think'. Sadhana reminds us of our innate relationship to Mother Nature. What is the point of yoga practice? Many people who come to a yoga class for the first time come for a physical benefit, to overcome injury or improve strength and flexibility – but these are just side benefits. The real point is to find ourselves closer to Spirit in all forms, to go deeper into life and stop skimming the surface. The practices of yoga asana (the physical poses) actually have a special power (siddhi) in them, which I have noticed unfolds in even the most hardened cynic given enough time. In yoga asana practice a hardening or calcification in the body and mind starts to dissolve and a psycho-kinetic transformation takes place as the body moves with the current of breath (life force or holy spirit) flowing through it. This is the internal practice that Pattabhi Jois, founder of the Ashtanga Yoga system speaks of. On the outside the body is moving, the breath is flow-ing; on the inside radical change is happening, deep transformation, breath by breath.

'Yoga is an internal practice. The rest is just a circus.'
– *Shri K. Pattabhi Jois*

The application of sadhana in everyday life works in a similar way. Sadhana means 'conscious spiritual practice', and it really has little to do with what you're doing on the outside and everything to do with what is going on inside. Just like the asana practice, when our daily lives embrace sadhana radical change starts to unfold. For example: you might be drinking a cup of tea; you're rushing around because it's morning and you're trying to get out of the door; you're looking for your keys and packing a bag as you gulp the tea down. The outer action is 'drinking a cup of tea', while the inner experience is fragmented and disconnected. If you were to drink a cup of tea as sadhana it would be a completely different experience. There would be mindfulness. You would give the tea your full attention, sitting quietly and enjoying the taste and warmth. There would be gratitude and elegance in your approach, such as we see in exquisite Japanese tea ceremonies.

Sadhana can be applied to anything you do that is uplifting and elevates your intention beyond the mundane or selfish. Sadhana is always anchored in *ahimsa* (non-violence, or kindness), because for a practice to be spiritual – filled with spirit – it must not harm another. We know this because we know we are ultimately all one. The Buddha explains this in his teaching of the 'web of life', often depicted through Buddhist iconography such as the 'thangkas' created in Tibet. As yogis we might call it oneness of being. We know about this web of life in our hearts, not our minds. If you eat a steak, some part of you knows you harmed not only the cow but your own spirit. It might not be conscious, but the knowing is there.

Spiritual practices help us to get closer to the knowing (intuition) of our own intrinsic kindness and compassion. This is why generally the practices get easier the more we apply them. They become second nature, or really an unfolding of our true nature that we forgot or have buried because of the non-conducive cultural conditions around us. We can replace those cultural conditions with *satsang* (spiritual community) by making our homes sacred spaces and by seeing all who we come into contact with as opportunities for satsang. Satsang, or creating spiritual community and friendships, brings the quality of compassion into action.

'On the surface, we appear separate from our surroundings, but under the surface there is a connection that binds us all. Similar to how on the surface embroidery appears separate from its background, but underneath the surface it's all connected.'
— *Alan Watts*

At this time in history and in our culture the application of ahimsa means to step up more than ever and remember our power as spiritual warriors. Now is our time, the time that kindness and compassion are most needed. We shouldn't get caught up in thinking that our efforts must be heroic or awe-inspiring. We can make a difference in the everyday – it is in the small moments of the everyday that transformation takes place. It says in the Bhagavad Gita, the ancient scripture from India named the 'Lord's Song', that if we offer something as small and unassuming as a leaf or a flower to the Divine in humility and love, that offering will be accepted and rewarded. It's not about grand gestures but rather patience, persistence and kindness in the small moments.

As a child I sang in the choir of my local church, which was a small, very traditional, beautiful but cold and musty building in the village I grew up in. I loved that place because it was the first sacred space I ever went to regularly, the first temple. My favourite Christmas carol that I remember from these times is *The Little Drummer Boy*. It tells the story of a poor child who goes to see the baby Jesus in Bethlehem but has nothing to offer so he plays his drum, and baby Jesus smiles at him. This is sadhana in action. Our task is as simple as picking a flower or two, lighting a candle and filling our homes with the sweet smell of incense or natural oils and devotional music. Make some fresh herbal tea. Sit down and journal your dreams and wishes for the year, keeping it simple and kind. Ask yourself, 'How can I give more?', 'How can I step up?' Our efforts do not have to be perfect, which is why we call them part of a practice in yoga. For me, more patience, less distraction and more presence are clear goals at the moment, especially with my young children. I wish to sit in wisdom, the vast world of intuition, dreams and mystery; this is to live in yoga.

The practice of ahimsa, non-violence, is a practice of alchemy. Alchemy means to transform one substance into another, usually more valuable substance, for example, turning base metal into gold. Through the practice of ahimsa or non-violence we transform not only ourselves, but the world around us. The ancient saints and sages who developed and codified the yogic practices we still do today knew this. They retreated into quiet spaces such as caves and forests to get very still and grounded in order to figure out how alchemy was possible. They realised that we are all part of one energy; we are all one thing together – separateness is an illusion.

They called this realisation 'enlightenment'. But they also knew in their great wisdom that it would be very difficult for most people to feel this connection, as most of us feel we are separate. So they made a suggestion: start with being kind. This is the secret formula to fixing almost any problem. Kindness is the magic ingredient that makes alchemy possible, turning lumps of lead into gold. Through the practices of yoga – starting with ahimsa – we start to see the oneness of being in the world. We stop seeing ourselves as separate. My teacher Sharon Gannon explains it like this: 'Yoga practices alchemically transform our perception of who we are. The body of the enlightened yogi houses the light of truth. The yogi lives in the world as an instrument for this truth. There are many yoga practices that can guide a person along the way to that magical remembering of who he or she really is.'

## The practice of bhakti

Narada was an enlightened sage from ancient times who offered his sacred teachings through kirtan, or devotional song. In Narada's scripture, the Bhakti Sutras, he outlines a four-stage process for developing *bhava*, or true devotion. Narada goes into a great deal of discussion in his sutra around which path is the best for getting close to God or for attaining deeper advancement in yoga. He particularly explores the contrasting paths of Jnana Yoga, or wisdom seeking, with Bhakti Yoga, or devotional practice. In simplistic terms, we could think of jnana as the path of the 'head' or intellect and bhakti as the path of 'heart' or feeling. In my own personal experience both are needed to progress, but the bhakti (devotional love and feeling) is most important and unfortunately many of us place far too much value on thinking to the detriment of this bhakti connection. Regardless, Narada places his emphasis on bhakti and gives us some clues as to how we might develop what he beautifully describes as a 'dynamic spiritual magnet of love in our hearts'.

## Narada's four-step plan for bhakti

1. Worshipping state of mind (puja): the essence of this first stage is in ritual or remembering our connection to the Divine through sacred action.
2. Praying state of mind: prayer is our conversation with the Divine.
3. Meditative state of mind: in the meditative state of mind we start to move out of longing and into a state of deeper connection. The journey moves from effort toward grace.

4.  Mind merging with the Divine: this stage requires no effort and is the manifestation of grace arising through previous effort.

'Inquire and investigate into what or whom you are truly devoted to. To what or to whom do you allocate most of your energy? Explore how this investigation can give you clarification as to whether your actions align with your aspirations.' – *Rima Rabath*

Narada's teachings remind us that progress on the spiritual path is not all up to us. We apply effort and at some point (who knows when; that is part of the mystery!) grace will arise. The effort is applied though the practices of puja, prayer and meditation. The rest is a process of swaha, or letting go, offering up your efforts to something higher than personal gain.

If you have never done a puja (devotional ritual) practice, start very simply. There are some beautiful ideas and instructions in Radhanath Swami's book *The Journey Within*, but you could start with simply lighting a candle, burning some incense or making a small sacred space in your home such as on a windowsill or mantelpiece. Place some sacred object there along with images of your teachers and perhaps a fresh flower. Honouring this space is the beginning of puja, and having such a space in your home will transform it.

Next the invitation is to pray. First you've got to know what you're praying to, but don't get too caught up in that. If you think you need a very clear image of God and a philosophically reconciled understanding of what God is before you start to pray, you might never get started! Let go of the need to intellectually understand and just pray, somehow to something. Even if you are cynical that God exists or feel silly, what is the harm in trying? I was taught to pray as a child in the Church of England, and my form of prayer to this day remains quite traditional. Sometimes I imagine I'm picking up the telephone and speaking to God, downloading all that's going on in my head, particularly my spiritual struggles, and being patiently listened to by a very wise and very kind friend. I also find my daily mantra recitation practice (japa) is a method of prayer. When I pray I ask for a lot of things; I'm petitioning. Ninety per cent of what I'm asking for is an increase in my own positive qualities. Often I ask for more patience or to be kinder. I ask for the clarity to act well and with skilful discernment. I never ask for material things, because I feel that my needs in that department are more than taken care of and it's a waste of treasured prayer time. It's actually a distortion of what prayer is to ask for 'stuff'; very few of us really need more stuff. I don't subscribe to the school of thought popular in manifestation circles that it is all right to ask for a Ferrari or diamond ring if that's what you want. That's a waste of your precious time with God. Ask for something that will actually make you happy, such as a peaceful heart or the ability to help others.

I've also stopped asking for understanding. I used to spend much more time petitioning God for understanding, as in 'help me understand why this person is so annoying to me in this situation', or 'help me understand why I am so frustrated'. But I realised even when the understanding came it didn't help me much. Now I focus more on shifting negative and unhelpful mental states and actions: 'help me let go of my frustration with him and reconnect to him', or 'help me dissolve my frustration back into Your love'. This is a much more productive and transformative way to pray. Knowing the 'why' doesn't always help cultivate the shifts we need. Sometimes the why is helpful because it helps us to shift a pattern or habit, and for this psychotherapy or counselling can be useful for unpacking the why skilfully. But it only goes so far – therapy without bhakti can be emotionally draining and limited in its power. At some point we all have to surrender to God, hold our hands up and let go.

When you get good at prayer you'll start to go much deeper in your meditation practice; it just happens without trying. If you begin a practice of prayer every day you will automatically be more drawn to meditation. For me, my meditation practice is like brushing my teeth or drinking water: it is an essential part of my life and it happens automatically. The practice of prayer has overlapped with meditation so that it is much easier for me to drop into connection to Krishna's grace even in very mundane moments such as standing in line somewhere or falling asleep at night. One of the biggest blocks to maintaining this telephone connection with God is, ironically, your mobile phone. If every spare moment of quiet or 'boredom' is filled with scrolling on a screen, you miss precious opportunities to reconnect, to pray, to meditate. These moments can happen multiple times a day. Reciting a mantra might help you to quickly connect (that's like dialling God's number – it's a quicker way to get through!). For many years I avoided social media and smart phone distraction; it served my meditation practice deeply to do so. These days it's become more of a struggle, and I do find myself drawn to Instagram instead of prayer (even just habitually) and to scrolling instead of just sitting. I see it as a truly toxic problem, and I'm working hard to put very clear and limited boundaries around my phone use. I encourage you to do the same, especially if you have young children; look at their faces, not your phone.

If you don't know how to begin to pray, try using the same words each day. This is a translation into English of a beautiful Sanskrit verse you could start with: 'May all be happy. May all be free from sickness. May all look to the good of others. May none suffer from sorrow.' This prayer extends out not only to human people but encompasses animal, tree and sea people, elemental beings, Mother Earth and all the caretakers of the universe alike. When we broaden our perspective of what a person is our circle of compassion expands; we extend our own experiences of being and might begin to see the Divine Self in all. Use the English words for prayer when you start. You can add Sanskrit mantra later when you're more practised or when you need to really drop out of your head and into your heart, but this happens more at the merging stage and japa (reciting a mantra using mala beads as a focus) can help with that. In the prayer stage we need some cognisance. In the beginning you want to connect with the intention of the prayer, praying as a petitioning and conversing with God in your own language. After prayer Narada suggests engaging in meditation practice.

## Simple guidelines for meditation

♥ Find a comfortable sitting position. Use a cushion under your buttocks and a wall or chair behind your back if needed. It will be difficult to meditate if you are distracted by discomfort in your body, so do all that you can to be set up to sit comfortably. Your spine should be as upright as possible, and ideally you won't lie down as this may make you too sleepy.

♥ Close your eyes, focus your attention inside and become still. Resist the tendency to fidget. It is usually a good idea to decide beforehand how long you will meditate for (ten minutes is a good start for beginners). You can set a timer and commit to being still for that amount of time.

♥ Bring your attention to your breath. Notice the inhalation and the exhalation as they enter and leave your body. You can focus on the tips of the nostrils where the breath enters and leaves the body to help you do this. Another good focus location in the body is the place between your eyebrows. As you sit in quiet stillness holding the focus in mind you will notice all kinds of thoughts coming and going through your mind. Try to let the thoughts flow through; don't hold on to a particular thought and build a story around it. Your breath will constantly flow through your body and your thoughts will flow through your mind. In time and with practice your thoughts will slow down and become less distracting. This is the beginning of the process of meditation. It's a lifetime's work, so don't get disheartened if it takes time to calm your mind in this way.

Narada's final step is the mind that merges with the Divine. What a wonderful promise, that we could walk in beauty and divinity all the time in all situations. Even in really difficult and dark situations, God would be with us and in us.

## Shiva and Shakti: divine masculine and feminine

We've reflected a lot already about God and the balance of intellect and effort with devotion and grace. Let's just pause for a moment and explore a little more deeply these two paths, which could also be described as the balance of masculine (yang) and feminine (yin). I firmly believe that gender exists on a spectrum (as does sexuality) but I do acknowledge some general differences between men and women, and at the risk of throwing myself into controversial waters I'd like to offer some thoughts on this big and important subject. I realise my ideas are not fully formed but more representative of my thinking on a difficult topic I'm still actively reflecting upon.

There are many organisations and lineages where men are still given precedence over women. The Catholic Church, Muslim faith and Hinduism all exalt man's place in spiritual hierarchy over woman's, and those religions alone are subscribed to by a huge chunk of the world's inhabitants. It is easy to get a little black and white (and therefore offended) in the unpacking of these teachings, but I believe there is huge benefit in also looking for the subtlety so often present below the surface. For example, I have found in my years of studying scripture that often meaning gets lost in translation. Sanskrit is a rich language of poetry and philosophy, and sometimes when we translate it into English we lose the subtlety of a specific choice of words or even the whole intended meaning. Hare Krishna devotee and elder Visakha Dasi helped me here:

> There are different types of intelligence and in Sanskrit there are many different words that are translated as 'intelligence'. One is 'buddhi', which refers not to a person's IQ but to his or her ability to discriminate, to be analytical. This is associated with male intelligence. But another Sanskrit word for intelligence is 'medha', which refers to mental vigour and power, nourishment, prudence and wisdom. Medha means 'the intellect illuminated by love' and is associated with female intelligence.

Many spiritual leaders and thinkers are making a distinction between men and women, which in its very nature endorses a binary perspective I'm not totally on board with. But what if instead of thinking about men and women we took these teachings and applied them through the lens of masculine and feminine, which could apply to all genders and manifestations of gender roles? It may not be what the traditional teachings wished to convey, but I believe yoga is a living tradition and I wonder if perhaps we can reinterpret the men/women conversation as a masculine/feminine conversation. There may be some pearls of wisdom here that can serve our spiritual goal, while still allowing us to put fixed gender ideas to the side.

This possibility is contained within the teaching of Shiva (divine masculine) and Shakti (divine feminine). The literal translation of Shakti from Sanskrit suggests an association with the idea of power. Shakti, far from being airy-fairy or less than her male counterpart in any way, is the power of creation. She is the rage that arcs up against injustice, especially injustice towards the more vulnerable members of a community such as animals or children. She is the inferno in your belly when creativity strikes and energy (prana) rises like a firecracker. She is the force of creation found in many places, including for some within the womb of a woman's physical body. She is all this and yet different to the Shiva or masculine energy, which is all about goals, linear thinking and external images and solutions.

Unfortunately, for far too long our dominant global culture has been anchored in the masculine. Here is one example: we've used the Shiva or yang approach with our Western medicine model, which disassociates us from our own healing and leads us disempowered to doctors and hospitals. There is a need to explore other ways of generating a healing paradigm for disease on the planet and in our own bodies and it lies in a swing back from Shiva to Shakti, from being healed externally back to self-responsibility.

I am not saying that doctors and hospitals are not needed – far from it – but that we need to each be engaged and actively participating in our own health and well-being. That is why my teacher Maya Tiwari called one of her books *Women's Power to Heal Through Inner Medicine*. She was recognising that much of the healing we need physically and on other levels is latent within us in the form of Shakti's grace. We've just crushed it with Shiva. This Shiva energy gets stuff done, but when unchecked and wild it will manifest war, destruction and greed. Shakti's job is to temper Shiva's vision, to cool things off and balance, which works well if Shakti is honoured and respected. If she is negated and suppressed, problems can arise on both the macro and micro levels.

On a global level the imbalance is seen in the rich getting richer and the poor getting poorer, the divide between the two getting larger and the numbers more and more horrific, where 1 per cent of the world's population own over 90 per cent of its resources (wealth). That's Shiva gone crazy. Shiva is also a little vain and all about the show and not so much connected to depth of feeling. That's why many of us have grown up thinking that shopping will make us happy and meditation is difficult. We've got things the wrong way around: when we get anchored in our Shakti, meditation is a gift, a joy and a guiding light. We know the value of getting to know our inner landscapes and clearing the rubbish out of there so we can experience the pristine mental states that are the truth of who we really are. We learn that a new car, a new house or a new pair of shoes will not lead to lasting happiness.

God is within each one of us; a little tiny piece of Krishna's love is right there in each of our hearts, somewhat buried and covered in dust perhaps but there nonetheless. When Shakti and Shiva energies are in balance we illuminate that jiva or individual soul shard of God. In the koshas model this is the bliss body or anandamaya kosha; we will look at the koshas, or layers of the self, in

Chapter 7. Patriarchy has done a great deal of damage to women's ability, in particular, to access this part of themselves. The goddess has been marginalised in favour of a more masculine form of the Divine that is incomplete and therefore difficult to access. We've been led to feel that our bodies are dirty, especially if they are menstruating, breastfeeding or otherwise Shakti-filled. Women who are empowered and who are raging against spiritual suppression are often labelled as 'mad' or given names like 'witch' as a form of insult.

'If you study yourself as a sample, a little sample of God, then you can understand God. God and we individual souls are of the same quality. It is the quantity that distinguishes us. Just like we have got creative power and God has also got creative power. By your creative power, you manufacture an airplane to fly in the sky, but by God's creative power, millions and trillions of planets are floating in the sky.'

*– Srila Prabhupada*

How to come back into balance? This is such a complicated question, and one I have contemplated for many years in my own life. One thing I've worked out is that the answer is not for women to become Shiva. I've seen lots of women do that in an attempt to fight patriarchal suppression, and it's exhausting. Trying to be both Shiva and Shakti simultaneously, taking on both roles all of the time, leaves us with a lot of energetic rubble to unpack. Instead, a fluid interchange, a dance, is needed. I think, I know, that empowered Shakti is the way forward. We can be carers, parents and guardians; we can be feminine; we can work in different ways and redefine social norms and role models; and because gender exists on a spectrum it should go without saying that this energetic paradigm is available to all of us.

## Ways to heal and strengthen Shakti prana

As a central understanding of the feminine power in Wise Earth Ayurveda, Maya Tiwari introduced the principle of 'Shakti prana' to the world. If you feel that your Shiva prana is low, figuring out how you can be more direct, clear and on target in your life and daily interactions will help you to engage with a masculine power that is healthy and helpful. However, it is usually the Shakti and not the Shiva that's disconnected for both men and women in our culture. Shakti is supported by cultivating compassion, slowness, softness and nurturing qualities. The following list will give you some more ideas:

♥ Experiment with and explore gender archetypes. The masculine and feminine role models can serve all of us at different times and in different ways and both have their beauty. Hone and use both your buddhi (discrimination, analytical mind) and your medha (intellect illuminated by love). Become both god and goddess, sacred lover and beloved.

♥ Observe and connect to the shifting energies of the moon; notice how you feel at new moon and full moon junctures particularly. This can connect to and support menstrual health for women. If you are a woman in your fertile years, healing your menstrual cycle is a big step to reclaiming your Shakti prana. See Chapter 4 for more on this subject.

♥ Practise ceremony. When we step into ceremony or heart-felt ritual we step out of autopilot and narrow thinking. Start your day with ceremony by lighting a candle and praying before you do anything else. End your day with ceremony by chanting mantra or journalling what you are grateful for before you sleep. See Chapter 7 for more on this subject.

♥ Smoke cleanse your space (with sage, incense or palo santo) then sit in meditation.

♥ Rethink your approach to healing when you are unwell. Experiment with aromatherapy and herbs rather than turning straight for pharmaceuticals. If you have mental health issues, look at a holistic rather than medicated method for healing (in consultation with a qualified naturopath or holistic GP).

♥ Connect to the season, land and people around you. Notice which foods grow seasonally where you live and eat those foods. Explore seasonal rhythm and cycles.

♥ Connect to the stories of your female ancestors. Talk to those who are still alive and ask about generations that came before. Particularly talking about the family history of birthing babies, spiritual awakenings and traditional family folklore around food and medicine are healing for Shakti prana. Be open minded and non-judgemental about which family members you ask and what they tell you. These are the stories that formed you, whether you like them or not. Sometimes a little reflection and deeper investigation of ancestral patterns can hold great riches of understanding for our own healing and evolving if we stay kind and expansive in our approach and thinking.

♥ If you are a man, one of the best ways to strengthen your Shakti is to develop or strengthen communication skills. Becoming a good listener to both your own emotions and feelings and to those of others is a great first step. Focusing on listening and being rather than problem solving or advice giving nourishes Shakti.

♥ Receive regular body work such as massage or acupuncture.

Part of what will heal our planet at this time is a redistribution of Shiva and Shakti and a healed and integrated balance of both in all human beings.

# CHAPTER 2

# Cultivating a sacred outlook

*Some suggestions for your conscious spiritual practice*

Life is not happening to you, rather, you are in control of how you experience the moments that make up your life. Once you start to live in this knowledge your life will begin to flow and be filled with positive synchronicities and blessings; you will experience the sacred in even the most mundane occasions.

## The purpose of sadhana

It may be useful to remove yourself from your everyday life once in a while in order to focus on your spiritual progress. Many religions and philosophical teachings advocate a 'retreat' from daily life to restore and refresh, as it is important to take time out of your life and relationships once in a while to reflect. Going on a journey or a retreat, and the change of scene this involves, usually inspire realisations and give us time for intensive spiritual practice; think of Catholics going on a pilgrimage to Lourdes or the Muslim Hajj to Mecca. However, the real work of our spiritual lives happens in the daily mundane moments, and this is our opportunity to practise sadhana every day.

'The world is violent and mercurial, it will have its way with you. We are saved only by love – love for each other and the love that we pour into the art that we feel compelled to share; being a parent, being a writer, being a painter, being a friend. We live in a perpetually burning building and what we must save from it, all the time, is love.' – *Tennessee Williams*

Ayurveda means 'wisdom of life', and is a traditional Indian set of teachings for health in body and mind. My teacher Maya Tiwari (Mother Maya) from the Wise Earth Ayurveda school has restored the original meaning of sadhana as 'actions that reclaim the Divine within'. Sadhana is conscious everyday activity that replicates the sacred in nature and so brings us in harmony with the great cycles of the cosmos. The goal of sadhana is to enable us to recover our natural rhythms to realign our inner life and daily habits with the cycles of the universe. When we begin to live and move in rhythm with nature, our mind becomes more lucid and peaceful and our health improves; life becomes easier. Sadhana brings us awareness of our inner harmony, and when this happens our power of intuition becomes active. We become more expressive, more fully alive and more in tune with our bodies and all our healing energies. Cultivating a sacred outlook through sadhana is essential to developing bhakti, or loving devotion, in your life.

The ancient yogic scripture of the Bhagavad Gita gives us three methods for keeping the Divine (Krishna) close in our hearts. The first method is to keep your mind and intellect steadily focused on the Divine; in other words, to remember at all times the yoke or yoga that binds us to universal consciousness or God. As Patanjali reminds us very early on in the Yoga Sutras, the mind is a monkey! It is very difficult to remain focused on anything for more than a few moments, let alone the Divine nature of all beings – especially when irritation and frustration arise.

We are given a second option if the mind is unfocused, if you are not able to keep your mind steadily on Krishna; that is to 'seek to attain Me by the constant practice of meditation' (Bhagavad Gita translation: Sharon Gannon, Chapter 12, sloka 9). Meditation is a tool to help us calm down the crazy monkey mind and remember our true nature and relationship to God.

What do we do if even meditation is elusive and difficult? We are offered a third option: to undertake all actions as an offering of karma yoga. When you make your life an act of seva or service you will remember your highest potential in all that you do, and in this way you will also remember your connection to God. This is how sadhana helps us so much. The reason I've focused so deeply on sadhana in this book is that it is the beginning of bringing spiritual practice into your life. If you don't wish to meditate as Krishna suggests in the Bhagavad Gita or make a puja as Narada invites us to in the Bhakti Sutras, you'll still need to eat and drink and perform the mundane activities that keep you alive. These can become sadhana, the start of your spiritual practice.

> 'If you cannot practise meditation, be focused on my work by
> performing actions for my sake, you shall attain enlightenment.'
> – *Bhagavad Gita translation: Sharon Gannon, Chapter 12, sloka 10*

Radhanath Swami, a bhakti yoga monk, describes this teaching beautifully:

> Bhakti yogis try to see the world through a spiritual lens and to
> perceive even material objects in ways that relate to the Supreme.
> By learning to love and serve God while living in this world we
> develop the eyes to see the world as it really is. Bhakti teaches
> us how to interact with the world through the strength of love.
> When our love for the Divine begins to awaken, it illuminates
> every aspect of our lives: the roles we play in family and society,
> our routines, our responsibilities and our relationships.

Although bhakti teachings encourage us to transcend the material world altogether one day (realising that ultimately we are Spirit and not the body we live in), bhakti yogis also feel the sacredness of the Earth and a sense of stewardship for what the Supreme has entrusted to them. So it is that the path of yoga encourages us to have a responsible social conscience and to be spiritual activists.

We have already discussed meditation, prayer, and service and devotion as ways of getting closer to a state of yoga. Let's look at some more options for cultivating sadhana and bhakti in your life.

## Dreams and the sleeping state

Observing and paying attention to your dreams is a tool for spiritual insight.

In the Yoga Sutras Patanjali suggests that our dreams can help us to connect to deeper spiritual awareness. Here are some dream practices you can try:

♥ Place a ritual object such as a crystal or affirmation card near or under your pillow and set the intention for dream awareness and memory as you fall asleep. As you fall asleep, ask your subconscious for a visionary dream.

♥ Breathe deeply in the dark as you are falling asleep. A connection to your breath starts the connection to Spirit. It is always important to the quality of your sleep to sleep in a dark room, so use an eye mask if your room is too light.

♥ Start a dream journal and write down your insights. Do this upon waking, otherwise you'll forget and your busy day-time mind will have a different memory and perspective from the sleepy mind. The mind when you are just waking bridges the conscious and subconscious, matter and spirit worlds more effectively.

♥ Read poems, fairytales, mystical stories and scripture before you fall asleep. Reciting mantra as you fall asleep can also be helpful.

♥ Keep phones, electronic devices and wi-fi out of your bedroom.

♥ Practise yoga nidra, or yogic sleep (deep relaxation) as you fall asleep or if you wake in the night and can't get back to sleep. This type of guided relaxation will help you carry wisdom from the dream state into everyday consciousness.

♥ Drink herbal tea before you go to bed. These herbs are all good for sweet dream states: rose, yarrow, sage, lavender and chamomile.

According to yoga master Sri Sri Ravi Shankar's interpretation of the Yoga Sutras, Patanjali states that our dreams can fall into one of five types. You may find it interesting to explore these in your journalling:

♥ unfulfilled desires are fulfilled (longing)

♥ intuition for the future arises

- ♥ you dream of the place you are in while sleeping (some people call this an out-of-body experience)
- ♥ stress release (past experiences) or anxiety dreams
- ♥ a mix of some of the above elements, for example, an anxiety dream set in the future

You will find as you practise active engagement with your dreaming you get better at it. Patanjali places a lot of emphasis on the dream states as well as the states of consciousness at the point of falling asleep, waking up and in yogic sleep. Each of these states can help us access insight about ourselves and the world and beings around us as we connect to them.

## The magical power of giving blessings

Here is a beautiful and powerful meditation given to me by my teacher Sharon Gannon that I have found to be of great benefit in my own practice:

Sit comfortably, close your eyes and become aware of your breathing, feeling each time there is breathing in and breathing out. Start with the people you know and love, as it is easier to give blessings to them. Silently say the words 'Blessings to …' as you inhale, and as you exhale say the name of someone. Continue for several minutes, extending your blessings to include your family and friends; then move on to others, such as your past boy- or girlfriends, neighbours, bosses and co-workers. Make sure to include others with whom you now have or in the past have had more difficult relationships. You will find that as you say their names their images will appear to you. With consistent practice over time you will be able to not only see them, but also to feel their presence when you name them. Over time difficult issues that you may have with them will begin to resolve themselves. Over time you will find that when they make an appearance in your dreams they will appear as benevolent, positive presences. Over time you will find that when and if you do encounter them physically, your relationship with them will have magically and dramatically changed. You will feel that there is a new ease in your interactions with them, and they will seem friendlier towards you. The feeling that they are coming at you will be lessened as your awareness of where they actually are coming from grows from inside of you. No matter how many good deeds you do or the many profound and intelligent words you may say, what people will remember most about you is how you made them feel. If you really want to live a life of service to others, it is helpful to learn ways to make others feel good. Learning how to give blessings in an anonymous way is a powerful means of transforming your world and the world of others. Because it is done anonymously you don't run the risk of inflating your ego, which could happen if you were to give the blessings in person.

Sometimes I use this practice as a brief form of prayer, especially if I see someone in my daily life who I cannot directly help; for example, walking past a homeless person in the street or a dead animal on the road. I will offer blessings to them silently as I walk by. I've taught my children to do this too, and it helps them when they see suffering and feel powerless about it. It is important to remember we are not giving blessings as an exalted being, as a guru would bless a devotee; it's a practice of cultivating loving kindness for all, as much for our own benefit (if not more so) than for the benefit of the recipient. If you know the Buddhist practice of loving kindness meditation, this meditation is similar in its intention.

## Pranayama

Prana is your life force or energy, and yama means to control or restrain. Thus pranayama is the control or restraint (channelling) of your life force, which is usually done by manipulating the breath. Pranayama shifts blockages on the mental and emotional levels and changes your auric field, or your 'vibe'. My two favourite pranayama techniques are very simple but very effective.

### Kapalabhati

This breathing practice, which consists of short, powerful exhales and passive inhales, is a traditional internal purification practice or kriya that tones and cleanses the respiratory system by encouraging the release of toxins and waste matter. It acts as a tonic for the whole system, refreshing and rejuvenating the body and mind. In Sanskrit kapala means 'skull' and bhati means 'light', so this practice is the skull-shining breath – or in other words, it brightens your sluggish head up! As you practise, you can imagine the lining of your skull being filled with the brightness of fresh new energy. I often like to practise kapalabhati in the shower in the morning, especially if I didn't have a refreshing night's sleep. My teacher David Life has referred to this practice as the 'yogi's cup of coffee' because of its invigorating effects.

Here is how to do it:

♥ Sit in a comfortable position where your spine is straight and your abdomen is not compressed.

♥ Rest your hands on your knees, palms facing down.

♥ Bring your awareness to your lower belly. To heighten your awareness you can place your hands, one on top of the other, on your lower belly rather than on your knees.

♥ Inhale through both nostrils deeply.

♥ Contract your lower belly or use your hands to gently press on this area, forcing out your breath in a short burst.

♥ As you quickly release the contraction your inhalation should be automatic and passive; your focus should be on exhaling. You are working towards a short, sharp (almost forced) exhalation followed by a relaxed and automatic inhalation. What is happening anatomically here is that your diaphragm (the umbrella-shaped large section of muscle at the base of your ribcage) is sharply forced up on the exhalation and relaxes for the inhalation.

♥ Begin slowly and gradually quickening the pace of the breath 'pumps', aiming for one per second. Always go at your own pace and stop if you feel faint or dizzy.

♥ After one minute of the exercise, inhale deeply through the nostrils, and then exhale slowly through your mouth.

Depending on your experience level, you can repeat the practice for up to five rounds.

## Extended exhalation

This technique is so simple it almost requires no explanation, but it is incredibly powerful. It works particularly well for people who suffer from anxiety or panic attacks. Quite simply, the focus is on extending your exhalation. The exhalation is the part of the breath that allows you to let go, to release tension, anxiety and even pain in the physical body. It is a good technique to try if you have a headache or menstrual cramps. It's also good for managing labour pain in childbirth. Chanting the primordial sound 'ommmmmm' is one way of extending your exhalation. Sometimes we do it naturally when we're frustrated (a sigh). Animals and young children often do a longer sighing exhalation as they transition into deep sleep. To go further with this technique, if you wish to increase Shakti energy, you can close off the right nostril and breathe in and out only through the left. This is good for pacifying tension, for example, if you were about to sit an exam. If you wish to increase Shiva energy you can close the left nostril and breath in and out only through the right. This is good for activating yourself and psyching yourself up for a task when energy is low. The left and right nostrils are the end points for two main energy lines (prana nadis) in the subtle body. The left side is *ida* (feminine) and the right is *pingala* (masculine).

# CHAPTER 3

# Mother Nature

*Eating with kindness and protecting the food source;*
*the mindful kitchen*

*Wise Earth Ayurveda's central practice of Mother Nature's Food Sadhana is presented in this chapter.*

## The kitchen as sacred sanctuary

The Upanishads are an ancient set of yogic teachings dating back hundreds of years. The Sanskrit word upanishad means 'to sit at the feet of', which I find such an evocative image for receiving spiritual teachings. Whenever I read or hear the word a beautiful image springs up in my mind of a group of humble students sitting underneath the shelter of a large noble tree receiving teachings from their holy guru. My favourite verse from the Upanishads offers a teaching about the value of all beings: 'The vital force which is this material universe and all it contains is equal to an ant or an elephant.' All living things are animated by prana, the life force of universal energy, and each individual is as necessary and valuable as all others.

We can compare this reverent attitude towards animals and the Earth herself found in Eastern literature with the modern-day image and attitude we find projected on to animals in the arts or on television. Mostly we are taught that animals are something to be used and that they are less than human. I was reading recently about the rate at which certain species are becoming extinct (for example, the koala population in Australia is only 20 per cent of what it was a couple of generations ago because we are destroying their natural habitat for industrial development). The impact of just one lost species has a huge knock-on effect on whole ecosystems, and the balance of the cycles of life and food chains. One example of this is that the decline in native bee populations means that much of our plant-based food sources are struggling due to a lack of pollination, and there are problems with fruiting as a result. Consider for a moment that without exception the only species whose extinction would benefit the planet is that of humankind. If human beings left the planet immediately it would have some chance of moving back into balance and survival, because sadly the way we are going leads us further and further into annihilation.

Underpinning our societies' ideas and perceptions about the value of animals is a value-based system that says 'we are better', when in fact we can see through many examples we are the problem. I offer this insight to encourage you to think about your relationship to animals as food. Factory farming and the horrors of animal abuse in the name of food production see animals as being ours to be used. The practices of sadhana cannot sit in alignment with this attitude. If we wish to practise sadhana in action, one key step is to adopt a vegetarian or vegan diet.

## Kitchen sadhana

My ayurveda teacher Maya Tiwari (Mother Maya) says: 'Food is memory. Eating is remembering.' This statement puzzled me for years: What do we remember? I came to understand in time that part of what we remember is our ancestral lineage, and that food connects culture and family. The importance of this is enormous in our communities, especially if the food is pure in nature and prepared with love. But the words 'eating is remembering' actually mean much more than that: it is a teaching that points to the memory an acorn has to become an oak tree, or the memory a baby has to inhale as she is born. When we eat wholesome and sattvic (pure) food we remember who we really are: compassionate beings born to be of service. We are custodians of the land and sky, and as such implicitly caretakers.

When food is prepared with loving awareness, we enhance the positive vibrations of the bounty nature has provided and remember our symbiotic connection to Mother Earth. In the practice of food sadhana we are awed by nature's intelligence, and we learn and improve our inner-medicine capacity for healing ourselves and maintaining balance on the planet. Sadhana practices see us in the kitchen grinding spices, kneading bread while chanting a healing mantra, building a devotional space and offering prayers and gratitude. These are not new ideas, but they may not be part of your current rituals and routines.

Sadhana is being present with everything we do, especially in the kitchen – the most sacred space in every home. It is considered as such because the greatest opportunity for blessings and nourishment can happen there several times each and every day. We are taught to use our hands (according to ayurveda the five elements course through our hands to each of our fingertips) to measure our food out. One handful of rice, for example, is called an 'anjali'. We also use our hands to knead and grind and prepare food so that the process of cooking is an all-sensory experience that connects us deeply to the food source itself. This is very different to unpacking something wrapped in plastic and putting it in a microwave! The sadhana kitchen minimises the use of equipment as much as possible, as the use of unnecessary electronics and electrical energy can easily tamper with the core vibration and energetic configuration (tanmatra) of nature's food.

What we do use are pots and utensils made of stone, straw, wood, crystal, brass and copper to remind us that these majestic materials are produced by the Earth and that cooking with them 'grounds' our food, maintaining the connection with the source of food as coming from the Earth. Using implements or kitchen items handed down through the family line is precious and, like our ancestors, we grow into reverence for the infinite number of gifts Mother Earth provides us. In this way, food preparation becomes first an offering to Mother Earth. This awareness sets the tone for investing our good and loving energy into the food. Food prepared the sadhana way teaches us how to live simply and love completely.

## Sadhana is a universal prayer

When we approach the sanctuary of our kitchen our very being becomes a *sankalpa*, a prayer. In our kitchens we can set an intention to heal the farmers, the land, the sky, water, air – to heal everything and everyone.

Sadhana is central to the principle of ahimsa. In an ayurvedic lifestyle we live close to nature and with the seasons, aware of the well-being of all of nature's creatures that surround us. Sadhana teaches us that wholesome food is the birthright of every person, animal and tree and that human beings are caretakers for that birthright (although we have lost our way). Healthy food created from the action of sadhana creates a healing body and serene mind.

Let me give you an example of food sadhana in action: the marriage of grains and beans. Maya Tiwari once described to me how she 'fell in love with the simple grains and simple beans', and these became a staple in her healing diet when she was recovering from cancer. She speaks of the marriage between different grains and beans in one-pot cooking. The combination of chickpeas and white rice is not good because of the difference in cooking time, whereas adzuki beans and brown basmati rice is a marriage made in heaven! The sizes of your grains matter, and the ancient grains were always smaller (think of millet or quinoa). I'm so fascinated by these very simple but powerful and practical teachings from ayurveda. Part of the process of seeing food as sadhana is simplifying our palettes, as we've become used to a rich array of multicultural and multi-ingredient cuisine. While that can be fun occasionally, it is bad for digestive health and robs us of the simple joy of simple food.

On the very special occasions when Mother Maya has blessed me by visiting my home and spending time with my family she has always cooked us the most delicious food that my boys can't wait to eat. I remember years ago she made sweet potato and millet for my oldest boy, and he talked about that dish for years! She will often pick some greens from the garden or soak some simple legumes, and with minimal spices and flavouring make something delectable. It was the same in her ashram in North Carolina when I visited her there. There is magic in food prepared with care, love and respect. This also brings to mind the stories of Srila Prabhupada when he first arrived in America in the 1960s as a penniless elderly man to spread the teachings of Krishna Consciousness. One of the first things he did was to personally prepare the vegetarian Sunday feasts for his followers; can you imagine how sweet that prasad (blessed food) must have tasted! These days millions of meals are served every Sunday at Krishna temples all over the world, from the seeds sown in that humble beginning and a desire to share the power and sustenance of blessed food.

## Setting up your kitchen in sadhana

Here are some guidelines for simplifying your kitchen in line with the protocols of ayurveda and sadhana:

♥ Have a sharp knife. An ancient vedic teaching suggests a sharp knife in the kitchen is good for not only preparing food but cutting through negative emotions and frustration so the food is filled with love.

♥ Avoid lots of what Mother Maya calls gizmos and gadgets. Keep your kitchen clutter free, and choose the best-quality utensils, pots and pans and crockery that make your heart sing. Most of my treasured kitchen items were either found in charity op shops or gifted from friends and family. My favourite item of all is my hand coffee/spice grinder that was handed down from my great-grandmother, who lived in Tyrol, Austria.

♥ When you are making big batches or doing physical jobs like kneading and grinding, if the mood takes you place a colourful cloth on the floor and work on the Earth. Even better, go outside for this work. Connection with the Earth joins us to our food in a special and unique way. Also, squatting while working in this way is good for your health and hips!

♥ Chant as you prepare food or play gentle chant music in your kitchen. Keep your kitchen clean and ordered. Offer a small amount of food to God once you have prepared it and before you eat it yourself or serve it to others. If you can, have a small sacred space with a tiny bowl and a candle in order to do this offering. You can say a blessing at this time or later when you serve the food. I use the Maha mantra for Krishna or a specific sloka (verse) from the Bhagavad Gita, which I share with you here:

> Brahmaarpanam Brahma Havir
> Brahmaagnau Brahmanaa Hutam
> Brahmaiva Tena Gantavyam
> Brahma Karma Samaadhinaa

This sloka reminds us that the source of our food, the food itself and the act of eating are all part of sadhana practice, and are linked to the perfect balance of nature and blessing from the Divine.

♥ Do not have lots of old, stale items in your fridge such as dated sauces or foods that last forever. They are devoid of prana.

♥ If you want to keep your food (and your mind) very sattvic and pure, avoid pungents such as onions, garlic, coffee and strong chilli. This guideline is especially good for those recovering from illness or going on spiritual retreat.

♥ Avoid damp and cold in your food. Do not add ice to your drinks or put out the digestive fire in your belly (agni) by drinking lots of water when you eat. Try not to eat food straight from the fridge.

## First, be kind

When we look at the problems in the world it is easy to become overwhelmed: we are destroying the environment, money is prioritised over health or ethics and wars rage. I feel powerless in the face of these problems, and my studies of politics only served to enhance this sense of powerlessness and also the feeling that many of the world's problems are so complex it is difficult to know where we could begin to find solutions.

An area where a huge amount of suffering happens on this planet every day is in factory farms. Millions of animals all over the world live an entire life of abject suffering in small cages where their basic needs and instincts are ignored. We are *not* powerless to create change in this area: every single time we eat we have a choice to either support this suffering or to boycott it and become part of the change we wish to see in the world.

A vegan (or vegetarian) diet is not always the easiest choice, and it is not always the choice most readily available or most commonly chosen by most of our culture and society, but it is a solution to one of the world's greatest shames and areas of suffering. So for me, choosing to be kind is my main food philosophy and all else comes second to that. It just happens to be a fortunate side effect that eating a plant-based diet is also very good for health and makes me feel great, as well as being the best choice for the environment!

Another part of being kind is to not be an angry or judgemental vegetarian. Not all of my family eats the same diet as me, so I try to educate and encourage but not to judge. Food should not become a source of conflict in your family. When our activities flow in the spirit of peace we invite the memory, energy and vibration of God within us.

Here are some ayurvedic food sadhana practices Mother Maya has recommended to me:

- ♥ Meditating on the full moon or the golden light of dawn before preparing food.
- ♥ Pounding the husks of whole grains or a blend of spices with a large pestle and mortar (I love to make my own chai tea in this way).
- ♥ Getting out of your head and into your hands. Connect with your true spirit by doing and not thinking. Put your hands in the soil or bread

dough and you will find yourself solving problems or having a creative breakthrough as a result of this hand-to-heart labour.

♥ Planting good seeds in the rich fertile earth. Ideally, grow and make as much food as possible yourself.

♥ Chewing grains such as brown rice in blissful serenity.

♥ Feeding your children from your own hands (anjali), not every day but as part of a loving ritual.

♥ Using local and seasonal food that is beautifully but simply offered.

## Family food practices

I'd like to share some of my family food practices to demonstrate some of these principles in action. Although we live in a city we have a growing food garden with lemon trees, a coffee tree, greens, root vegies, celery and lots of herbs. We have olive trees, and we preserve the olives (we get through a lot of olives in our household). My neighbours give us pumpkins, lemongrass, fresh root turmeric and again lots of herbs. I like to make as much of my own staple foods as possible such as stock, baked items and kombucha. I would like to add coconut yoghurt and masalas to that list in time. I also sometimes make prasad (snacks) for offering at the kirtans (chanting gatherings) I attend regularly, which I especially enjoy because prasad is an offering to others and to the Divine source. A big exception to my homemade efforts is green juice, which we buy at the farmers' markets every week because it is locally produced from organic greens grown close to our home and is not heat treated; it's delicious. It's a big time and mess saver for our big family to buy our large weekly juice quota in this way.

A sadhana I've recently started learning about is the collecting and eating of foraged food especially local weeds and medicinal herbs. Many weeds have a bitter flavour profile, which is one of the six tastes of a balanced meal according to ayurveda. In our Western food preferences, bitter flavour is often less popular or missing. Dandelion and rocket are bitters that are easy to grow. Harvesting and eating so-called weeds also reduces the need for chemical sprays to eliminate them. An interesting book on this topic is *The Wild Wisdom of Weeds*, by Katrina Blair. My mother-in-law used to gather a wild bitter green called hortha and make a delicious side dish with it.

'Sometimes eating just one petal from a wildflower can provide more sustenance than even an entire meal of cultivated modern foods. This is because wild foods feed us on a level that transcends the physical and reawakens our connection to the living world in a way that satisfies a deeper hunger. Our bodies recognize these wild tastes and textures and they awaken something ancient and powerful within us. When we receive wild nourishment, we step into a relationship of sacred responsibility and reciprocity with both the plants and the places which sustain us.' – *herbalist Sophia Rose*

Although I enjoy experimenting with making herbal tea blends, flower remedies, essential oil blends and other gentle medicinal herbal preparations to fortify health, when we live and eat in the sadhana way our immunity and health become robust. In ayurveda immunity is called 'ojas'; it is linked to so much more than just disease prevention and can be supported by all the factors of sadhana we've explored here.

I don't want you to feel overwhelmed by all these instructions. I dip in and out of focusing on different aspects of the sadhana kitchen in my own life and for my family. Life gets busy and I wouldn't want to paint a picture that implies I'm always in the kitchen baking fresh bread. In contradiction to the teachings on doing as much as possible by hand, for convenience I do have a Thermomix blender, which shortcuts a lot of processes. But like many elements of spiritual life, slowing down and becoming more mindful is a practice, a culmination of attention, intention and effort that reaps rich rewards.

These practices make sense and are an intelligent approach to living that has served millions of people over countless generations. It's relatively recently that we've begun to get it so wrong with our approach to food, and going back to the ayurvedic framework can help us remedy that. I'm reminded of a broader context teaching shared by a senior Krishna Consciousness devotee, Visakha Dasi, where she said: 'Prabhupada wasn't trying to impress us with his knowledge or seniority or even really to win us to his point of view. He was telling us what he perceived as the truth. He didn't speak directly to our issues but gave us a framework with which to solve them. And he did it without making us feel guilty or ashamed or foolish. He appealed to our higher nature – my higher nature – a nature he knew beyond a doubt we had.' If we are fortunate enough to have access to these teachings we have the framework. If we are blessed enough to have a spiritual teacher we have a cheerleader, someone who wants to see us heal and step into the action or karma of devoted life. Perhaps the final step is for us to believe in ourselves and love ourselves and our families enough to feel the value of this approach and make some gentle changes in the direction of solving some of the issues we face.

## CHAPTER 4

# Intention and manifestation

*Your thoughts, words and actions; your routines
and rhythms*

## Intention and manifestation

There is a beautiful word in the Sanskrit language that translates as something like a cross between a promise, a resolve, a prayer and an intention. The word is sankalpa, and making a sankulpa is a very powerful thing to do. A sankulpa always has at its core an uplifting ideal or spiritual value. It could be quite mundane and practical (for example, a resolve to give up smoking), or based in more profound values and aspirations. The most effective way to set a sankulpa is in the present as if it's already happened, for example, 'I am a non-smoker'. The most effective time to recite your sankulpa is when you are rested and relaxed, because in this way it will enter your subconscious as already real. This is why during the practice of yoga nidra (guided deep relaxation) a sankulpa is often suggested. If there is something in your life you wish to change, particularly a bad habit or behaviour, setting the intention to change is the first step.

Manifestation practices and intention setting are another way of thinking about living in your true dharma, or answering the calling of your heart to be of service in the world. The practice of manifestation will enable you to become a pro-active participant in your life, and to avoid the feeling that life is 'coming at you'. If you are unclear about your dharma or purpose in life or overwhelmed by choices, manifestation will help you. The intentions you set and the goals you wish to manifest will give you clues about what your soul is longing for. This process is useful for making decisions both big and small. There are a few stages to successfully setting intentions and this practice is best done at the time of a new moon.

## Setting intentions

♥ *Think*: the first stage is to get still and quiet in meditation and to notice what is going on in your mind. As your mind settles (the chitta vritti becomes slower and more stable) notice what stories, thoughts and dreams come up. See if you can consciously direct your thoughts towards what it is you are longing for spiritually. You can write these observations in a journal or notebook if you feel called to do so.

♥ *Feel*: get into your body. You might do this through some yoga asana or you may have another embodiment practice to bring energy into action so you can feel what is going on within you. Dancing can be good, or even receiving a massage. As you feel into your body, notice any blocks or areas of constriction that prevent the flow of prana. What can you do to release them? Consciously let go of tension in your physical body through breath, movement or touch and open up to feeling the subtle pulse of the Divine through your body's prana nadis (energy lines).

♥ *Commit*: stop doubting or comparing and stick to your chosen path, at least for a time. For example, maybe you've decided to give up coffee or alcohol consumption. Decide how long you will do this for and observe the results.

♥ *Act*: make some plans about what actions you will take to move towards your personal growth goals. What practical things can you say, think about or do to make your goals come to pass? Patanjali's ethical codes found in the yamas and niyamas might be helpful here to check in with making sure your goals and dreams are aligned with strong values. When we take steps in the right direction towards our dharma, even if they are baby steps, universal consciousness delights and comes rushing in to support us. This is where the manifestation practices become so powerful and where an understanding of karma is imperative. What you sow you will reap in thoughts, words and actions.

♥ *Have faith*: with our efforts firmly in place we relax into shraddha or faith in the Divine plan. Bhakti practices of chanting and devotional service help to cultivate shradha.

♥ *Live in dharma*: by constantly practising yoga, yoking yourself to the Divine and practising these steps to manifest your goals you cannot fail to live in your dharma.

I have mentioned already that I'm not a big fan of using these setting intentions techniques to manifest material gain or to feed unnecessary greed. I believe we should use this type of work to achieve our spiritual and dharmic goals so we can be of great use in the world and greater service to ourselves and others. A good example would be making a sankulpa to observe a vegetarian diet.

One of my favourite manifestation stories is that of Srila Prabhupada when he came to America as a penniless elderly man and founded the Hare Krishna movement. I also think of Ingrid Newkirk and her personal vision as an animal rights activist that led to the founding of People for the Ethical Treatment of Animals, now the largest animal rights charity in the world and an organisation for whom I am proud to volunteer. Both these individuals had an unshakeably strong resolve and vision that focused on being of service.

One of the reasons we might make a resolve or sankalpa is to help us to stick with our intentions, to be serious about them. There may be some tapas (fire, discipline) needed. The next step up from a resolve is a vow, which may be taken in front of a guru and could be part of an initiation process. A spiritual vow is a powerful karma to take on and could transform your life deeply.

'The vow of Ahimsa (non-violence) is much more than a vow, a resolution or a promise. It is a sankulpa. Like most Sanskrit terminology there is simply no equitable translation in other languages for this word. We could say it is a blessing or a sacred intention or intent that is held in the greater mind (buddhi) witnessed by the sakshi (inner witness), so that we are continually prodded by memory and prana to guide and remind us as we move along in our everyday rhythm. In this way we remember our vow when it counts. And when we forget to remember, we are consoled by the fact that our awareness is growing. Sooner or later we remember.'
– *Maya Tiwari*

*More than one million people across the world have taken the vow of Ahimsa, an inner harmony and world peace practice that was pioneered by Maya Tiwari.*

## Menstruation and the moon cycles

As mentioned, the best time of the month for setting intentions and holding space for your goals is new moon. For women, this will also be the time of menstruation if your cycles are in sync with the moon. Menstruation is the shedding, the letting go or release to make space for new possibilities. On a primal level it is the body clearing the way for the possibility of new fertility and conception of life. On an energetic level it is also a space clearing, a shedding of the old to make space for the new. You may think it a little archaic or pointless to be concerned about aligning your menstrual cycles with those of the moon. Consider for a moment that your body is made of over 70 per cent water. The moon has a huge gravitational pull on the bodies of water on planet Earth, and is responsible for the ebb and flow of the tides of any body of water. It stands to reason, then, that the moon's cycles and rhythm would also have an impact on our own inner cycles and rhythms, especially those that are so based in fluid and water.

'According to ayurveda, a woman's natural rhythms are kept and preserved by her monthly menstrual cycle that occurs with the new moon. At this time, menstruation is set in motion by the sun absorbing energies from the earth, which in turn draws the menstrual waste from the body. When we lose our relationship with the lunar wheel we just go around and around "spinning our wheels" in a way that is undirected, unfocused. We start to lose touch with the essential spirit of ahimsa and experience hurt, angst, despair or inexplicable pain. To reclaim our living ahimsa, we must re-establish our connection to the elements, moon, sun and the stars.'

*– Maya Tiwari*

Some of the elements that can disrupt this alignment of the menstrual cycle include toxic foods, the contraceptive pill and other birth control devices, stress and anxiety, suppression of the feminine energy (feeling like you always need to be in your masculine in order to compete or get ahead) and sexual trauma. Most women have experienced or are experiencing something on that list at some point in their lives. No wonder we are out of balance. How do we reclaim this rhythm and come back into our power as women?

The energy that will serve us in re-establishing balance is Shakti prana. Prana is energy or life force, and Shakti is the energy of the goddess. It is found in women in the lower two energy centres (chakras) around the belly and reproductive organs. The depletion of Shakti prana in our culture is demonstrated in the collective experience of depleted fertility, menstrual problems and hormonal disruption. When we talk about the goddess most people start to imagine something very gentle and calming. The alignment of menstruation with the moon sometimes manifests as a gentle and inward energy but is also sometimes fierce. I think of the goddess Kali, who is all fight and fire and has a garland of skulls around her neck. Sometimes the letting go requires fire in the belly, and sometimes calling in or manifesting change is charged with the fury of standing up to injustice or comes from a place where we get tired of our own laziness or weariness and are ready to stand up and act.

New moon energy is potent for activists too, not only for manifesting change and energy from which to act in the world but also for letting go of hurt and disappointment (the energy of full moon is good for working with forgiveness and is helpful in this way for activists and change makers too). At this time in history (or her-story) we need to call on our power and ability to step up. This doesn't mean masculinising or fighting; it means finding a new way, the way of what Maya Tiwari would call 'inner medicine'.

So many cultures, including Germanic, ancient Greek, Chinese and French, connect the woman's menstrual cycle with the moon and the power of the lunar cycle. By reconnecting to these cycles women can re-establish strength and Shakti prana.

## Ways to bring your menstrual cycle back into balance

♥ Observing the cycles of the moon and connecting to them. You can download an app on your phone to do this that will also allow you to track your menstruation in connection to the moon. Or, even better, you can go outside at night and actually look at the moon just as generation upon generation of women before you would have done.

♥ Taking a bath of rose petals and raspberry leaf (make a giant teabag using an old tea towel or muslin and soak the herbs in the water for a while before getting in). Do this on new moon days, especially if you are not menstruating in alignment with the moon. Light a candle, put on some beautiful and feminine music and make a ritual of the experience.

♥ Massage your belly with a base oil such as coconut or almond that has a couple of drops of lavender or clary sage blended into it.

♥ Set intention at new moon time, the time for manifestation. Take time to journal your goals and dreams. Write out the things you are ready to let go of on a piece of paper, especially anything you have been holding on to that makes you angry, and burn it or bury it.

♥ Sit with other women in a women's circle. Many women's circles are now popping up all over the world as women realise the power of coming together in supportive and kind community to nourish each other and preserve Shakti prana. If you can't find a circle in your area, there are also wonderful online offerings.

I have been amazed in the workshops and teachings I have offered on this subject how many women have told me their cycles have come into alignment through the simple practice of observing the moon. Attention and intention creates deep transformation.

'In Sanskrit, there are many words for moon. In Sanskrit poetry, a woman's beauty is said to be like the light of the moon. And in Yogic dialog, the moon that waxes and wanes is symbolic of the thinking mind. The moon has many meanings. The full moon in Yoga, is symbolic of awareness reaching its fullest expansion within you. Honour that moon force, honour the movement of the tides within you, honour that full moon within.'

— *Manorma*

## Daily routine

As well as observing and coming into resonance with the cycles of the moon, we also have a daily rhythm and set of routines and rituals that ayurveda calls 'dinacharya'. Dinacharya are your daily cleansing and health-promoting habits and include your routines around falling asleep and waking up and everything in between.

### Wholesome dinacharya suggestions

♥ Rising with the sun and resting when the sun goes down; this would be a great time to switch off all electronic devices if you have the discipline to do so! Likewise, do not start your day on a screen, and if you need an alarm to wake up let it be gentle and ideally not from your phone.

♥ Give yourself an oil massage before you get in the shower (abhyanga).

♥ As well as brushing your teeth and cleaning your body, cleanse your sinuses using a neti pot filled with saline solution.

♥ Lunch should be the largest meal of the day and ideally followed by a short restorative rest time.

♥ Yoga, meditation and pranayama practices are best done in the early morning and/or before bed. Ideally, you will be in bed ready for sleep by 10 pm.

> ♥ If there is any light in your sleeping area, wear an
> eye mask.

Routine of any kind will help to establish balance in your constitution. It will also balance your biological clock. Modern science is showing that human beings are losing connection to the circadian rhythms of night and day. This is extremely detrimental to health and is exacerbated by artificial light in our homes and environments, artificial blue light from screens and devices, shift work and jet lag. All of the dinacharya suggestions can help to rebalance this modern problem with ancient wisdom. Your dinacharya should not become dogmatic, and even if you are not able to maintain this routine every day you can do the activities that bring you the most benefit. As well as considering daily routines you may also take into account the cycles of the seasons in your activities, perhaps being more active in summer and entering into reflective hibernation in winter.

## Addiction

All addictions are part of the human tendency to avoid pain and to experience heightened states. Yogis believe these goals can be reached through spiritual practices, but this is a slow and steady path to take. Mind-altering substances (and other addictions such as gambling or even addictions to pornography or social media) offer quick and radical changes in a person's mental states.

Recovering from addiction means to embark on self-enquiry and repro-gramming back to a slow and steady approach of working with the mind. Of course, the guidance of a good teacher is imperative, and in my experience those best equipped to help an addict are recovered addicts themselves. I don't have personal experience in this area, but the reason I wanted to write briefly about it here is that I have witnessed many, many people in incredible transformation and life-saving recovery from addiction through utilising the practices of yoga, often in tandem with programs such as the twelve-step program.

Russell Brand, whom I love, wrote a brilliant book on addiction titled *Recovery: Freedom from our addictions*. He has an interest in yoga, which comes through in the book. He recognises the role of dharma in our lives, and the problems addiction creates for discovering and following our dharma, when he writes about recovering from addiction being a process of becoming the person you were meant to be. Addictions are like a heavy dark blanket that gets thrown over the truth of who we are, and in Brand's experience recovery programs and yoga practices have helped to lift that blanket off.

I also recommend Gabor Maté's book *In the Realm of the Hungry Ghosts* on the subject of addiction. He has studied the Bhagavad Gita and has worked in addiction recovery clinics as a medical doctor for decades. It's an incredible book full of insight, not only for addicts but for all of us to guide us to deeper understanding of our own tendencies toward addiction. Through understanding we can offer support and develop compassion rather than judgement for those around us who are struggling.

One of the ways in which the practices of mindful awareness and meditation can help with addictive tendencies is that they give us tools to be able to observe our own process of thinking and acting. We talk in yoga about 'thoughts, words and actions' because the ancient yogis knew that what you think will ultimately lead to what you do. We attempt to cultivate kindness in thoughts so that our actions in the world will reflect this. This is the opposite emphasis to what is usually seen as being important. Most people think that what you do is the most powerful, followed by what you say and finally by what you think, so that if a thought remains private it doesn't matter how negative or judgemental it is. Yogis know that by healing our thinking we can heal our actions – it works from the inside out. That is why working on yourself is never a selfish act; it is an act of caring about what you put out into the world.

Science has shown that the gap between a thought and acting on that thought is usually only about half a second for most people. This is called the 'impulse action synapse', and it occurs in the cortex of the brain. Usually the cortex also has the capacity for self-regulation, a kind of brake mechanism that in that half a second will kick in if we know the action will be self-defeating. This is where we learn self-restraint and skilful behaviour. It is a learning that happens from childhood into adulthood, where as we develop we are less impulsive. A two year old will scream and cry if her ice-cream falls on the ground, whereas an adult will take it in their stride. If as children we are not nurtured by adults to establish this type of self-regulation it will be more of a struggle as an adult. Some studies show that in addicts the mechanism that allows the cortex to suppress behaviour it judges to be unhelpful is damaged. This is why willpower is not the only part of overcoming addiction, and where learning to both observe and actively work with brain chemistry and function patterns are imperative to recovery. Meditation can help all of us to do this, to find again and extend the gap of awareness between an impulse and an action. It can help us to be more patient and less reactive, and for some it can also be a key in dealing with deep addiction.

'When you know yourself, then you will be known and you will understand that you are children of the Living Father. But if you do not know yourselves, then you dwell in poverty and you are poverty.'
– *Jesus Christ, The Gospel According to Thomas*

## Karma and samskaras

We have established that what you think, say and do matters. Let's look a little more deeply at why. Your thoughts, words and actions are creating your karmas. Samskaras are the subtle impressions of our past actions. As long as we are alive we continuously perform actions, but not all of them contribute to the formation of samskaras. Actions that we perform with full awareness are the ones that make the greatest impressions on our mind. In other words, it is the intention behind the action that gives power to that action. This process is beautifully explained by the literal meaning of the word samskara: sam means 'well planned, well thought out'; and kara means 'the action undertaken'. The roots of this word are also present in karma, meaning 'action'. So samskara means 'the impression of, the impact of, the action we perform with full awareness of its goals'.

You can think of samskaras as being like the grooves in an old-fashioned vinyl music record. It is through these grooves that the music is held and can later be played. The grooves are mapped in a certain way to hold the music. When we perform such an action a subtle impression is deposited in our mental field; our intentions matter in this regard as much as the outcomes. Each time the action is repeated, the impression becomes stronger, which is how a habit is formed. The stronger the habit, the less control we have over our mind and our thoughts when we try to change or break our habit patterns. We all have seen how our habitual patterns subtly yet powerfully motivate our thoughts, speech and actions. Samskaras can also play into patterns of addiction, and will form a stronger influence for some people than others. This is why, according to yogic teachings at least, some people are more prone to addictive tendencies than others.

If you believe in rebirth or reincarnation, the yogic scriptures tell us that samskaras can be carried through from one lifetime to the next. This helps us to explain how karma works and also why bad things sometimes happen to good people (because of karmas carried through from past lives).

## Re-evaluating what we really need and want

Mahatma Gandhi told us that 'there is enough in the world for everyone's need but not for everyone's greed', and yet we are not living as if that were true.

There is hope for humanity, but it will take diligent work. In the Bhagavad Gita, Krishna tells Arjuna that he has to fight his battles, that no one else can do the job for him. But to fight with a noble attitude and compassion on our side is to take action in which we can put our faith and trust. We are like Arjuna: we have access to Krishna's guidance through the Bhagavad Gita and we have the opportunity, now, to fight our own noble battles. At this challenging time in the history of our planet we can rest assured that mercy and compassion will manifest to bring balance if we work hard ourselves to bring these qualities into being.

Let's say all of your basic needs are taken care of. I'm guessing they are because I know by the fact that you are reading this you are literate and understand English, which already puts you in the top 38 per cent of educated world citizens. You also have time for spiritual reflection, which is in itself a great blessing and luxury. If you were a cow imprisoned in a factory farm or one of the many political prisoners incarcerated for speaking truth your most important battle might be for liberty. But again, you are reading this so I'm guessing you're not imprisoned. So what is the most important battle in your life? It is more than likely you have everything you need materially taken care of. Perhaps what you lack is the feeling of abundant time and maybe you also feel you lack power. Perhaps you lack trust in yourself and others. Perhaps, at times, you lack love and devotion and humility. That's the battle right there: finding those qualities so you can reside in bliss and breathe easy.

The Bhagavad Gita can give you some indications of how you can come to know you are abundant in everything, of how these battles might be fought and won. We are so fortunate these teachings are available to us when we most need them, so let us not waste this important pivotal moment in the human story.

The Bhagavad Gita talks about the idea of making a contribution or being of service a great deal. That will bring you to great happiness; that's what your spiritual journey in this lifetime is all about. It's not about anything more than serving others. We get very caught up in materialism; very caught up in relationships, hoping others will heal us rather than feeling complete within ourselves. We also get caught up in the ego identity that comes with a great job or a fast car or the way our hair looks today or whatever it might be. And Krishna says that ultimately those things will never really make you happy. There's another way: being of service is the ultimate way to sow seeds that will sprout into good karmas for you and others. All twelve-step programs such as Alcoholics Anonymous or Narcotics Anonymous also offer similar advice; namely, if you help others who have suffered as you have it will benefit your own healing.

Each of us, rich or poor, young or old, only has twenty-four hours in each day. And who knows how long we have left of this blessed lifetime in the vessel of this body we have been gifted? If you can take just one gem of wisdom from these teachings and apply it in your own precious life, the door will open to lifetimes of plenitude, calm and great fortune. Each one of us every day has potential to go into battle as Arjuna did and fight to be kind, compassionate and willing to do God's work. Arjuna's dilemma on the battlefield is a metaphor for our daily battles to practise yoga, the yoking of our small selves to Divine will. Krishna's strategy for peace and happiness in the world is simple and effective, but it requires your participation and resolve. You can begin in this moment.

## Trusted practices

'A mirror is meant to perfectly reflect our image when we look into it. But if it's covered with dust the image will be clouded or distorted, or we might not see ourselves at all. The mind is like a mirror. Over the years, we have allowed it to become covered in the dust of misconceptions, desires and fear. All these are born of a false sense of who we are. When we look into that mirror, we mainly see dust. Worse, we think the dust distorted image is a true reflection of ourselves.

Meditation on mantra helps us clean the mental mirror so we can see something true about ourselves – the pure soul we really are. As the mind clears, the fog of misconception fades, and the natural qualities of the soul emerge. We begin to feel the love that's inherent within us …' – *Radhanath Swami*

Some of our daily routines will make up trusted practices. These are the foolproof practices and rituals that we come back to time and again when all else fails or when we're too tired, overwhelmed, emotional or depressed to come up with anything else. Sometimes the trusted practices are difficult to do because we don't feel able to do anything, but do them we will and invariably we know they will help to shift whatever funk we're in. Trusted practices are like the simple family dinners that I fall back on when the fridge is bare or my energy is low; for me, this is usually some kind of minestrone soup. Actually, minestrone soup is a good analogy for trusted practices: a little bit of this, a little bit of that, which can be found without digging too deep, some tried and tested simple additions (salt, oil) and it's usually quite tasty. Not life changing, but perfectly nourishing.

Your tried and tested practices will be your own; they will develop over time and repetition. The point is in doing them, even when you feel you can't. They are not necessarily spiritual practices in the formal sense, but they are energy shifters.

## Suggestions for trusted practices

♥ Indulge in a quick body scan or ten-minute relaxation (I usually lie down with one hand on my heart and one hand on my belly and practise conscious deep breathing).

♥ Dab some essential oils on your wrists.

♥ Choose a sloka or sutra from scripture and spending five minutes journalling on it.

♥ Light a candle and clean your sacred space, picking some flowers or leaves and arranging them as an offering.

♥ Make a cup of tea and drink it quietly with an uplifting book or piece of scripture.

♥ Practise a few sun salutations, some mantra recitation or a little pranayama. The Jivamukti Magic Ten sequence is perfect for a short practice.

Every time you repeat a trusted practice over and over it is like a mantra, an affirmation, a spell. Part of my trusted practices is also to remind myself that often what I am worrying about is transient and not deeply important. It's mundane reality issues, or what Prabhupada called 'transient coverings' rather than my true spiritual nature. Remembering God and dedicating my efforts to a higher purpose help me to reconnect, and the best way I know of doing this is to recite mantra.

'Prabhupada urged us to focus on our spiritual nature and not on the soul's transient coverings. He encouraged us to engage in spiritual activities – bhakti – by dedicating our minds, words and body to Krishna's service without material motivation. Only in that way, he said, would we find lasting happiness.' – *Visakha Dasi*

## Japa

By far the most powerful trusted practice of my own life is japa meditation (mantra repetition) using mala beads. In my opinion, this is the most powerful teaching I can possibly share with you. Often bhakti yoga practitioners will decide on a minimum number of mantras they want to chant each day. The main purpose of the beads is to keep track of the number of mantras chanted. Feeling the beads move through your fingers also engages your sense of touch and helps to focus your mind on the activity of chanting.

There are 108 beads on a mala strand and one larger bead, known as the guru bead or Krishna bead. For meditation purposes, it is good to use a string of beads where all the beads are the same size and made of the same material, which will promote a consistency of experience as you are meditating. Begin with the bead next to the Krishna bead. Gently roll the bead between the thumb and middle finger of your right hand while chanting. Try not to use your index finger, as this represents ego (the finger you point at people when you're telling them off!). You can chant a mantra of your choice, but it's good to stick with the same one for months or years. I use the following mantra:

> *Hare Krishna, Hare Krishna, Krishna Krishna, Hare Hare*
> *Hare Rama, Hare Rama, Rama Rama, Hare Hare*

Prior to using this mantra (known as the maha mantra or great mantra), which I switched to about a year ago, I used a different mantra that my teacher gave me:

> *Shri Krishna Sharanam Mamah*

I chanted this mantra every day for over ten years. These are Krishna mantras, but you could choose a different mantra that appeals to you. It could be English, for example, 'may all beings be happy and free', or a short Christian prayer. This process is not much different to how Catholics use rosary beads for the Hail Mary. For each bead recite your chosen mantra once then move forward to the next bead (pulling the bead towards you, into your hand) and repeat the mantra.

In this way, continue chanting on each of the 108 beads in the strand until you again reach the Krishna bead. This is known as one round of *japa* and usually takes from six to ten minutes. Once you reach the Krishna bead do not go over it but, rather, turn the mala around and go back the way you came until you've completed your designated number of mala rounds. It is also possible to do japa practice without mala beads, and personally I've trained myself to practise japa as I fall asleep and as I wake up. I used to do this with beads, but since I've been co-sleeping with my babies I stopped using the beads as often I'd fall asleep using them and I worried they would get tangled up with the baby as we slept!

It is a good idea to keep your mala beads in a special bag or pouch just for them, to keep them clean and to keep the energetic vibration around them pure. You shouldn't wear the mala you use for meditation as a piece of jewellery and you should try to always use the same mala for meditation. It is said that when your mala breaks you've shed some big karmas and it is time to get a new one (a big energetic fresh start). You can also keep your mala on your altar or sacred space if you have one. I keep mine next to my bedhead in a small bag beside a picture of Mother Mary and Ganesh. You may ask your spiritual teacher if you have one to bless your mala beads, and if you undergo initiation into a bhakti lineage your guru will give you new mala beads as a part of this process.

## Making sacred

If you don't even have the time or capacity to do any of the above practical exercises, or you're in a place where it's not possible (like on the bus, or in the supermarket), it can be a trusted practice simply to check in with what your mind is doing. Calming what Patanjali called the 'chitta vritti' (whirlings of the mind) and cultivating kindness in that space is a profound act. It is in what might sometimes feel like the daily grind that old wounds and stories often appear and reappear and we can get really stuck. This feeling of daily life being hard is often best shifted with simple pleasures – a ritual insurance policy, something that you can fall back on and retreat into if only for a moment. My teacher taught me to breathe in and mentally, silently, say to myself 'let', then breathe out mentally and silently say 'go'. This can be done anywhere at any time. It's available to you as a tool rather than another more self-destructive pattern or story that you might turn to in challenging moments.

In her book *Fierce Medicine*, which is a truly pioneering piece of work, yoga teacher Ana Forrest dives deep into the topics of addiction, self-abuse and low self-esteem. She too discusses in length her own versions of the trusted practices that have served her and the many hundreds of yogis she has taught. I especially like her practice of tuning into whatever body part it is we are holding a negative story or thought in. Is it manifesting as tension in your neck, a knot in your belly, a tight jaw? Once we check in we can begin to soften and most importantly stop holding on so tightly.

Through awareness, healing begins. And in softening our grip, especially the grip on things we have absolutely no control over, healing begins. The types of practices I'm describing are those we don't have to carve out special time for, go on retreat to do or be in a special circumstance or head space to embrace. They are not special, but they *are* the most special because they are done sitting at your desk on a rainy Monday afternoon, or when caring for cranky young children, or when your friend or your partner has hurt your feelings with an unkind comment. These trusted practices are the magic of everyday life, the spells and incantations that get us through in busy traffic or tiresome meetings. Although seemingly mundane these practices, through time and repeated application, can become more than the sum of the parts – they truly take on an energy of their own and become siddhis or magically powerful.

## Yogic siddhis

A few years ago, my teacher Maya Tiwari gave me a book to read written by Corrie ten Boom called *The Hiding Place*. Ten Boom, who was Dutch, survived Nazi occupation of her country. She was a devout Christian who along with her family helped to hide and protect many Jewish people during the occupation. In the book, we hear of what I can only describe as many yogic siddhis (I think Corrie ten Boom would have thought of them as miracles).

In one, a Jewish man who has a terrible breathing disorder and is very noisy with every breath through day and night manages to become quiet when the Nazis are searching for him and only inches away from his hiding place. In another, Corrie is sent to a concentration camp and has with her a small jar of vitamin C powder. She describes how that jar was never discovered and confiscated, seemed to go on forever and literally saved the lives of many. At first she thought to keep it for herself and her sister only, but when she shared it the jar just kept replenishing itself.

A miracle ... or what the yogis would call her siddhi: her magic arising as a result of her elevated consciousness and kindness. Patanjali talks a lot about the siddhis in Chapter 3 of the Yoga Sutras. Sometimes they can be a distraction (flights of fancy such as levitation) that take those gifted with them further from spiritual development because ego and pride start to swell, but others are gifts that can serve and contain the sparkle of a miracle.

Having a bag with you that contains a few items that might help you do your work in the world as you go about your daily business could be a wonderful sadhana. Corrie ten Boom felt more violated by having her bag containing her Bible and a few medicines taken from her than she did by anything else that happened in the camps. This was her toolbag for serving others. I like to carry lavender oil with me wherever I go as well as a small felt star on a string, which is useful for calming down fractious children or making a bond with shy ones whom I meet. My teacher Sharon Gannon carries birdseed in her handbag to feed wild birds, especially in city parks where they are often hungry.

I also have a doula bag packed for when I'm called to a birth as a birth assistant. This contains remedies such as arnica and rescue remedy, but also a warm clean blanket, nourishing snacks, gentle essential oils, a crystal and a few herbal teabags. With this bag, I feel I'm ready to support a woman as she goes through the rite of passage that is birthing a baby. Of course, I could do so without the paraphernalia, but the gifts these carefully selected sacred objects offer me are profound. When I was running my own yoga studio, I noticed that often the yoga teachers travelling the world who came to stay with me and my family would set up a small altar in their sleeping space with a few special images. It was devotion on the road. Mystic and teacher Milla, of Fireweed and Nettle, says of her tarot cards: 'I carry my cards everywhere. They are like a ritual insurance policy, a personal soothsayer, something to offer folks I meet, a little piece of home away from home.'

When I lead a women's circle I have a basket containing my special tools: my mandala floor cloth, candles, notepaper and pens for journalling, a vase for freshly picked flowers and a crystal that was a gift from a friend. These are the precious items that enable me to make a sacred bhava and are deeply valuable to me as a space holder.

Our special sacred items are wonderful tools for our spiritual work. It is also a good practice to not get too attached to 'stuff' and to improvise where needed. When I feel like I'm lacking something material that I 'need' I think of the Tyagi yogis in India – wandering sadhus (spiritual practitioners) who have renounced all material possessions to the point they have no clothing and live naked even in cold weather.

## Life, death and everything in between

'The first thing you will do when you come into this life is to inhale.
The last thing you will do as you leave your body is to exhale.
What happens in between is the precious opportunity of a lifetime.'
*– Sharon Gannon*

The guru mantra that I used as the dedication for this book reminds us to honour all our teachers. The first teacher we are invited to honour is 'this life I have been given'. That includes an honouring of all the people who made your life possible, including your biological parents and the people who were present at your birth. Honouring our birth parents is part of healing the first energy centre in the body, the base chakra. As a doula (birth-support person), I find it such an honour to serve women as they birth their babies and to aid in creating sacred space for new beings to enter the experience of life.

Just as we honour the moment of life starting, so too yogis honour the moment of the end of life. In fact, in the births I have had the honour of witnessing I've always had in the back of my awareness a quite visceral and unexplained sense of death as well as birth. It sounds morbid but it is not at all; it's actually quite joyful. It is almost as if when I've watched babies being born, an experience I find incredibly moving, I also somehow sense there are other souls at the same time in other places leaving their bodies. It's like a big energetic sliding doors experience of birth and death, and somehow I feel the connection of many souls coming in and others going out deeply in the witnessing of these events.

Some yogic practices ask us to prepare for the moment of death, and I believe this can be an enormously beneficial practice. Patanjali says in the Yoga Sutras that fear of death is a huge stumbling block or hindrance to progress on the spiritual path. Part of our work as yogis is to accept and even embrace the fact that one day we will leave this body. Your body isn't yours; it is only on loan. The practice of breath retention on the exhale can help to prepare us for the moment of death. Usually if you ask someone to hold their breath they will take a big inhalation and then hold. It feels uncomfortable to exhale and empty the lungs then hold the breath out, because when you die the last thing you will do is exhale. Getting used to it now might help you in the moment of death to be ready, even if that moment comes unexpectedly. Pranayama practices that involve holding the breath out such as uddiyana bandha can help you prepare for a graceful death.

If you have practised japa meditation diligently throughout your life you may also find your mantra comes to mind in moments of struggle as well as in the moment of death. When he was assassinated by gunshot and fell to his knees on a crowded street, Gandhi famously uttered his mantra in his dying moments. I found my mantra spontaneously arising as I naturally birthed three of my children. With my last child I was in much more extreme pain than I had been with the others and the mantra disappeared. This tells me I still have some work to do!

# CHAPTER 5

# Precious life path

*Discovering your life path and honouring your family ancestry*

The ancient Vedic scriptures tell us that we have chosen our lives and, specifically, our parents and the culture into which we are born. Your spirit-soul chose to incarnate into this particular place and time in order to purify specific karmas. For this reason, honouring, healing and celebrating our ancestry are important practices for anyone wishing to progress spiritually.

## Personal ancestry

As my own spiritual path has unfolded I've found myself coming back to my own ancestry as well as drawing deeply from the well of yoga and Eastern spiritual traditions. My ancestry going back a few generations is in Celtic and pagan traditions and these speak to me deeply, although in essence I recognise that the wise people in all planes of time and space are yogis. This is what makes yoga not a religion in itself, but simply the yoking of the self to God. That happens outside of cultural context or individual conditioning although it may be informed by it, meaning that in many different traditions and ways we can potentially 'yoke' with the Divine.

Although I've been a yoga teacher for many years and have spent a lot of time in India, I sometimes find the stories and mythology of Indian culture less resonant than those of my ancestral heritage. For example, as a child I was drawn to Romany and gypsy stories, and as a very young girl I had a friend at school who was a gypsy whom I would beg to tell me the stories her grandmother had shared with her. These were the stories of the land I grew up on, the hedges and forests I knew, and they were alive for me. Now living in Australia for many years I enjoy the Aboriginal stories of flora, fauna and animals indigenous to this land. Yoga teacher Ana Forrest and her partner Jose Calarco have done some beautiful work weaving Aboriginal stories into ceremony and sharings, as well as even making up some new Australian-inspired yoga asana such as 'emu' and 'ostrich' sequences.

We have access to so many different teachings from so many different lineages and the world is getting smaller and smaller. On the one hand, I see the importance of tying ourselves to one tradition and sticking with it, of seeing a process through. It's easy to swap and change our spiritual calling if the going gets tough or if any austerity is required. If we do this, we will never go deep enough to have a breakthrough; hard work is needed. However, on the other hand, to limit ourselves to one teacher or one set of teachings seems to me needlessly restrictive. Perhaps as with so many dilemmas a middle ground is helpful – discipline and connection to one path mixed with a healthy balance of outside influences and creative flair. Cultural appropriation can be a symptom of spiritual longing for those of us who have grown up in a society that overly emphasises the material.

My teacher Mother Maya has taught me a great deal about the importance of honouring my ancestors and how to do this. I've been blessed to be guided by Maya in ceremony for honouring the ancestors. These ceremonies are something you can try at home as part of your own healing journey.

'You have a choice to create elegance and self-healing out of the muck of your lineal patterns, genetics and neuroses. That revelation occurs when you don't isolate the sacred to only what is convenient or positive or looks good.' – *Guru Jagat*

Yogi Bhajan, the guru who brought Kundalini Yoga to the West, said that our subtle or energy bodies are impacted by the seven generations that came before us. The modern scientific investigation into epigenetics confirms this type of patterning, and tells us that we all carry genetic coding from our grandparents and earlier generations that goes above and beyond simple

DNA structures. It seems that genetics is far more complex than we first thought and all kinds of threads are impacting us from generations past, which means that all of us are holding some trauma and some patterning from part ancestors. Fortunately, we have the tools to work with this and heal. This work goes back to the concept of samskaras; we have the chance to rewrite the music on our vinyl and let go of patterns and karmas from the past that are not serving us. We may also remember elements of our ancestry worth celebrating and cultivating.

## Chakra balancing

Sanskrit is such an elegant language with so many words for concepts like 'love' and 'God' that we lack nuance for in the English language. The word 'ego' is a good example of this. The Sanskrit word for ego is 'ahamkara', and it relates to the idea of the individual self that facilitates life's journey. Ahamkara generally has a positive spin on the idea of ego: it is the sense of self we need in order to have a vessel to grow and learn with through life. However, in the Yoga Sutras Patanjali uses a different word for ego: 'asmita', which he describes as a hindrance to spiritual development. Whereas the ahamkara encapsulates the sense of self that contains enlightenment potential or self-realisation, Patanjali takes a different stance on ego and says it binds us or hinders us into self-identity. The application of asmita sees us attaching to statements such as 'I am Katie', 'I am a mother', 'I like chocolate'. We are bound and restricted by these statements of self-identity and they stunt spiritual growth.

We also need to be aware of the influences on the ahamkara that are not our stuff. These influences manifest physically, emotionally and spiritually, and can come most strongly from our parents and then flow back in time through ancestral lines. Our bodies are made of rivers of subtle energy (prana), in Sanskrit known as *nadis*. Where nadis meet and intersect we have chakras, or energy junctures, of which there are seven main ones. Working with the chakras can help us to balance the relationships in our lives and the prana in our body in order to purify the ahamkara and the ancestral lines as well as the karmas we are generating ourselves. The ahamkara can be purified by working with your prana. I recommend Sharon Gannon's *Chakra Balancing* DVD for a guided practice that does this work very specifically and deeply.

---

## The seven chakras

Here is a list of the chakras and the corresponding relationships for each:

- ♥ muladhara (base): parents
- ♥ svadhishthana (below navel): creative, business and intimate partnerships
- ♥ manipura (above navel): others you have hurt
- ♥ anahata (heart): others who have hurt you (forgiveness)
- ♥ vishuddha (throat): yourself (seeing yourself as a holy being)
- ♥ ajna (third eye): your teachers/guru
- ♥ sahasraha (crown of the head): God

Using the magical blessings meditation (see Chapter 2) for each of these relationship areas and breathing into the corresponding area in your own body at the same time would be one way of beginning this healing work.

## Cultural ancestry

I live in Australia, which raises an interesting question in terms of ancestry. Although my childhood was spent in one place on the planet I now live somewhere very different. As we all travel more and the world gets smaller, our cultural ancestry and the ancestry of the places in which we find ourselves living all play a part in our spiritual journey. There is a need not only to celebrate diversity, but to deeply honour and respect each other's lineages and history. Yoga, ayurveda and Aboriginal spiritual teachings all honour the intuitive realm and suggest that if we become quiet enough in ourselves, through meditation or through spending time living close to the Earth, healing will take place. The Aboriginal word *bulwalwanga* means 'we are strong', and points to the ideas that our nature and our birth rite is to heal. Even the seemingly insurmountable problems faced by contemporary Aboriginal communities and by the environment of the land I live on here in Australia, which has been disseminated by modern farming practices and poor environmental planning, has the potential to be healed.

Sydney-based ayurvedic teacher Shaun Matthews puts it like this: 'The ancient Yogis and the Aboriginal Elders of Australia both knew the same thing, that our essential nature is peace. This gets obscured by the conscious and unconscious mind but the peace is there, part of who you are, from conception until the day you shed your physical body. The wisdom traditions of India and Australia both know this.'

The rishis in India had an acute observational sense and learned from the land and animals around them. We need only look at the names of the yoga poses to see this: we learn from the form of the tree and the mountain and the snake and the lion. The Aboriginal people had this same ability to learn from the natural world around them, a practice which they call 'the listening'.

Almost all cultures globally have been impacted now by Western or modern industrialised culture and paradigms. In her ground-breaking book *Ancient Futures* written in 1991, author Helena Norberg-Hodge writes about her time in Tibet and the influence of Western culture there. She observes that as with many so-called traditional cultures, there is an admiration of the ease of Western living and the material comfort we enjoy. However, she also acutely observes the areas in which contemporary culture spreads a toxic environmental and cultural disregard – this was almost 30 years ago!

'Westerners implicitly compare traditional cultures with the ideals promised by development and ignore the reality of what development has brought to societies around the world.'
– *Helena Norberg-Hodge*

I think it is important to remember this when we travel. For example, on a recent trip I asked myself as a white, Western yogi travelling and learning in India, how could I be as respectful as possible and engage in an enriching reciprocal dialogue and exchange for both parties? This is the challenge of a shrinking world. One solution lies in waiting to be invited to participate in traditions that do not form part of our own cultural heritage. This was part of the blessing from Srila Prabhupada in bringing Krishna Consciousness to the Western world: he actively invited us on this path. If it is not possible to travel to your ancestral lands, then hearing stories and maintaining some traditions from them is the next best thing.

Recently I've become more sensitive to the challenges of cultural misappropriation. This is in part because of the deep interest in Indian spiritual teachings I am describing, which are not part of my ancestry, and in part because Australia is an entire continent of land stolen by my ancestors from the Aboriginal people. I am aware that Caucasian people freely use in their everyday lives objects, rituals and symbols that are sacredly important to ancient cultures. For example, it could be considered 'playful' for a white man or woman to cover his or her face with tribal markings, but this negates all the suffering and loss of destroyed generations. I do not feel it is acceptable for me to paint my face in a tribal manner because it's playful. In the same way, I would discourage my children from dressing up and playing cowboys and Indians.

It could be argued that in the spirit of oneness of being it's acceptable for us to all exchange cultural reference points. For me to bow to Ganesh, to henna my hands, to dance an Aboriginal dance or climb a sacred mountain might be acceptable in the spirit of oneness of being because we are all one anyway and we can all do as we please. In using this statement in the context of dialogue around cultural appropriation we have to be very careful not to negate oppression and racial prejudice. Are we all refugees? Are we all animals in factory farms? Do we all experience prejudice, discrimination and hate campaigning on a daily basis? As a white, middle-class female I can honestly say my experience is one of deep privilege and ease. I would not offend the Aboriginal Peoples whose stolen land I live on by suggesting we are 'the same'. I'm clearly entitled and privileged and free in ways that 99 per cent of the other human beings on planet Earth at this time are not.

Cultural appropriation also extends to the use of symbols and imagery. The use of symbols such as the Sanskrit alphabet, the sacred mantras and even the power of the written word are of enormous importance. Humankind lives and dies by our flags, our totems and the intentions they convey. Think of the Nazi flag or the Om symbol: these evocative images are important and deeply meaningful. I am not suggesting we cannot chant mantras or use appropriate symbols from diverse cultures; I have Sanskrit tattoos on my own body. But I do believe firmly that the conversation about cultural appropriation needs to be had and that it is relevant in my own life in the two arenas I've mentioned: the land upon which I live, which is Aboriginal land, and the practices I have dedicated my life to, which are Indian in origin.

If we wish to respect everyone and celebrate everybody's contributions to our evolution we can only do so once old wounds are healed. In some hopeful and beautiful visioning of the future, perhaps a time will come where all cultures are equally respected and celebrated. We are not there yet.

If you do find yourself inadvertently causing offence or unintentionally perpetuating stereotypes, the best thing you can do is to acknowledge your error and apologise. Once we know better we can do better. It diffuses tension if you make people feel they have been heard, respected and honoured, especially if you have caused offence.

I love the writing of Arundhati Roy on this topic, as she looks from a slightly different perspective at the issue of globalisation and the monoculture that corporate dominance creates. She suggests that globalisation doesn't have to mean the end of cultural diversity, and that in fact the best way to resist corporate institutionalisation is in multiplicity and the celebration of diversity. She says that the best way to resist homogenisation is with 'the dismantling of the Big – big bombs, big dams, big ideologies, big contradictions, big heroes, big mistakes. Perhaps it will be the century of the Small.'

Our private spiritual practices and creative pursuits in our own homes and communities are part of this dismantling. The food we cook, the unique clothing we wear and the music we make are all opportunities to dismantle the Big culture of corporate domination. Every time you make an item of clothing or a beautiful meal or write a poem it is a protest against the negative impacts of globalisation. What could be more intimate, more personal and more individual than your relationship with Spirit? No corporation, dictator, historical or political movement can take that from us; history has proven it to be the most robust of entities and ultimately this relationship always manifests as a personal expression.

Much like the debates on gender and interpreting the scriptures and yogic teachings for a new generation, which has a less binary vision of gender, I see this topic of cultural appropriation as an ongoing area of reflection for me. I feel that I am only loosely beginning to understand the subtleties of this subject, and I'm far from reconciled in my own positions. Sometimes I feel disconnected listening to stories of Ganesh and Hanuman and relate more to fairytale stories of figures such as Baba Yaga, which connect more to my personal ancestry. At other times I feel a visceral pull to the Indian teachings (from past lives I am sure, but that is a whole other conversation and one that puts a totally new spin on cultural appropriation). At this moment the best I can do is be respectful of all cultures and ask permission where appropriate.

## Small steps towards healing the past

The wounds inflicted upon ancient cultures in the last few centuries have been enormous, and it is easy to feel that healing is impossible or that change cannot happen. But from small acts of change, profound change can be nurtured. The following suggestions could be a beginning:

♥ Have a representation of the land's original culture in schools that is historically honest and culturally sensitive. Education delivered in the right way can break down prejudice.

♥ Review the national anthem. For example, Aboriginal people were neither new to Australian lands nor free when Australia's anthem was written, so perhaps an anthem that reflects reconciliation would be more appropriate.

♥ If you are a teacher, sharing an acknowledgement of country at the beginning of each class would be a respectful beginning to the practice. These words could be used: 'I acknowledge the _____ peoples as the first peoples of this nation and pay my deep respect to the Indigenous custodians of this land on which we meet today. I pay tribute to the Elders both past and present and hope that in some small way my teachings assist in the custodianship of this land. It is a great privilege to be standing on country.'

♥ Work within communities and with existing elders and leaders rather than imposing solutions from the outside without community consultation. For example, ideally yoga classes taught within Aboriginal communities would be taught by Aboriginal teachers. If you run training programs for teachers, you might consider an

Indigenous person's scholarship offering within your local community.

If you live in a country with First Nations people you can adapt these suggestions to your own context.

We must make space for our differences and closely guard our lineages and heritage. If the Big takes over as the world gets smaller languages will be lost and traditions eroded, and before we know it we will all be drinking Coca-Cola and wearing jeans and t-shirts. It is our job to keep the beauty of the Small that Arundhati Roy describes. In due course reconciliation and healing can happen in both small ways and in big ways, but so also can preservation of culture and evolution of culture that is respectful and intact rather than hodgepodge and eroded. For example, yoga is a living, breathing possibility as alive in the Western world as it is in India. We are guardians of these teachings, and each of us as yogis has a responsibility to listen to all voices and consider our own narratives within those voices and whether we are serving or diminishing with them.

## Ancestral storytelling

'Deep memory is awakened through ancestry – it is the essential pre-recorded history of our cumulative passages through all time.'

– *Maya Tiwari*

Maya likens the unfolding of our ancestral line to beads on a mala, each one connected yet separate from the rest. We may be unable to remember our ancestors with our cognitive memory, but in what Maya calls the 'hidden mala of the heart-self' we can awaken intuitive powers that can unlock both the hidden trauma and surprising beauty of karmas that have led us to this lifetime.

Let me give you a very simple example. I am a doula, which means I support women when they are birthing their babies. When I first meet a woman I am going to work with we go through a process of getting to know one another and I ask lots of questions. These questions are both practical and personal in nature. I might ask about what fear is present for her around childbirth and what types of interventions she anticipates she might or might not need. But by far the most powerful questions are around the matriarchal birthing lineage. 'How did your grandmother birth?' is a question many of us might not even know the answer to, but there are gems of wisdom in those questions. Is there a feeling of safety and joy in the family history of birthing? Is that the energetic thread carried down through the generations? Or was there war, fear, ill-health?

Superficially we might not think these stories impact us now but they do, and very deeply and not just in the area of birth. In fact, our ancestors' stories are our stories and they form part of the tapestry of who we are. A wonderful older Christian Sister midwife I met once at a conference (who herself has four children) described how when souls come into this life, sometimes they are not sure if they want to stay; the baby is in ill-health. She said: 'I give them a firm talking to. "You chose this family, you chose this body, you chose this moment – now commit to it! Breathe! Come into this life" and, whoosh, they enter the body!'

In knowing our stories we also come to know the celebrations from our ancestral line as well as knowing there is always a chance to begin again and break negative cycles both in ourselves and in our family history. In Jonathan Safran Foer's book *Eating Animals* he begins with a story about his Jewish grandmother, who experienced starvation during World War 2. It is a moving story in which he describes how she wouldn't eat pork when it was offered to her even to save her life, because she said: 'If nothing matters then there is nothing to save.' This story stayed with me for years after I read it. It is a beautiful and inspiring story of deep dharma, deep respect for ancestry, and also shines a light on how the past influences and impacts the future in good and frightening ways.

'Be not the slave of your own past – plunge into the sublime seas, dive deep and swim far, so you shall come back with new self-respect, with new power, and with an advanced experience that shall explain and overlook the old.'
– *Ralph Waldo Emerson*

The truth is that we can't be free of our ancestry, especially where karma is heavy. This means we all have work to do in healing for our ancestors. In our home, we have a special sacred space for the ancestors close to my altar and the place where we sit and eat. The ancestors live with us and are kept alive in us. Looking at images of your ancestors and honouring them is one way of healing past wounds. So, also, is talking about old family stories and asking elders in your family for stories of your past.

'Wisdom sits in places. It's like water that never dries up. You need to drink water to stay alive, don't you? Well you also need to drink from places. You must remember everything about them. You must learn their names. You must remember what happened at them long ago. You must think about it and keep on thinking about it. Then your mind will become smoother and smoother. Then you will see danger before it happens.'

*– Native American Chief of the Chiricahua Apache people*

Sometimes our ancestry is held in the vibe of a place: a room, a church, a sacred space in your home. This is where burning sage to create smoke and space clearing can be important.

'Honouring your ancestors is the first step in reclaiming your spiritual heritage. As you begin to recover your ancestral memories, you will also uncover unconscious, troubled memories that prevent you from knowing the truth of who you are. According to the Vedic sages, we humans are the only species which has the power of intuition. Yet too easily we forfeit our sacred birthright and with it the ability to change and grow, create, and strive for inner freedom. We have largely forgotten the joy, love, and wellness that are intrinsic to human nature.'

*– Maya Tiwari*

## Healing your ancestry

This practice is derived from Wise Earth Ayurveda's education, which recognises the need for ancestral healing in our world. Introduced by Maya Tiwari more than 30 years ago, this ancestral vedic practice was previously an elaborate set of ceremonies performed only by Hindu priests and men, and was simplified into a universal practice accessible to every man and woman in the world.

Here are the ritual steps to creating healing harmony for your ancestors and breaking their patterns within you. Before you get started, gather black sesame seeds or uncooked rice, water, a large bowl and a jug. Create a quiet and sacred space where you will be undisturbed.

Write down as many of your ancestors' names as you know.

- ♥ Place a small handful of black sesame seeds or uncooked rice into the bowl. Try to use black or wild rice if possible.

- ♥ Fill the pitcher with water.

- ♥ Sit in a comfortable posture on the ground, inside or outdoors – and face south.

- ♥ Mix more rice or seeds with the liquid in the bowl.

- ♥ Create jnana mudra with the thumb and forefinger of your right hand touching in a circle. Pour the liquid mixture through the mudra and into the bowl. Recite the names of your ancestors aloud as you pour.

♥ Take the liquid outdoors and sprinkle it as an offering for wild birds and animals. Some birds such as crows are considered to be symbols for our ancestors. Notice which birds come to feed and how they behave. Do not discard the mixture in the garbage.

♥ Sit in stillness for some time and repeat the phrase 'may all my ancestors reside in peace and freedom', either out loud or silently. You could recite this phrase 108 times using your mala beads. Stay mindful of your ancestors known and unknown. Pray for their safe travel in the celestial sphere, for their entry into the abode of the peace, and for their well-being and nourishment.

This ritual releases the ancestral energy that's deeply embedded in our tissues, freeing us of the need to re-enact their memory patterns. You may want to do multiple sessions of healing to free trapped energies.

## The magic of kindness

Karma embodies a very complicated set of teachings. We all know that karma does not manifest instantly in all cases. Seeds can lie dormant in the earth for many years before the conditions are right for them to sprout into seedlings, but the law of karma states that eventually and inevitably those seeds will sprout. Be careful what you sow.

'When you are unkind to someone you plant a seed to see unkindness. For example, you judge someone as a greedy person. As soon as you think or say that, you plant a seed that will insure that greedy people will appear in your life. When you see yourself as poor, as not having enough to be able to share and be generous to others, you plant seeds for seeing yourself as a victim of poverty and that will become your reality as you continue to nourish that perception of yourself.'

*– Sharon Gannon*

We know that just because we wish for something or practise seeing something (such as a person) in a certain way doesn't make it so – except that sometimes it does. Let's say you don't like your boss much but you practise seeing her in a kind light. You look for her good qualities and point them out to others; you respond with kindness when she is impatient or harsh. You may see your relationship with your boss shift at this point and no longer be so difficult. This is a likely outcome of your efforts, but it doesn't always work in terms of changing relationships; sometimes we have to try other strategies. One thing is always true, though, and that is that by only ever having a kind and loving response to others you are not accruing bad karma for yourself – you are not sowing any rotten seeds.

'Once you realise that the world is your own projection you are free of it. However is the picture, beautiful or ugly, you are painting it and you are not bound by it. Realise that there is nobody to force it on you. See the imaginary as imaginary and be free of fear.'

*– Sri Nisargadatta Maharaj*

Magical thinking often works but doesn't *always* work. Sometimes we have to walk away from a situation or a person because it's toxic or abusive or because we can't be of help, which is where our discernment comes in. Practising sadhana in your life will help you to awaken intuitive awareness about when to push and when to let go, when to fight and when to step back. You will know what to do because you will be grounded in your own body, confident in your gut. It takes time to develop that confidence because our current culture doesn't support it. We're encouraged to look to others or to the church or to pop psychology or even to celebrities as role models and advisers. I want to encourage you to look within. Some tools will help you, such as asana practice, meditation, sadhana and sitting in sacred space. If you're open to it, affirmation cards and shamanic visions or dreams, which are all just tools for opening the portal to your inner knowing, can also help. Remember how much faith in that inner guide Patanjali puts in the Yoga Sutras. He encourages us to work with our dream states for guidance and advice. He is totally down with the magical effects of our efforts in spiritual practice, but emphasises they should be used for our own ascension towards enlightenment and not for cheap tricks and showing off.

## Shift your vibration

If you are feeling a bit flat or overwhelmed, try one of these practices to shift your vibration:

♥ Practise seeing your current state in the context of the wide arc of time. Nothing is permanent, and it is likely you will not have the same worry in a year or even a month's time.

♥ Take some time in your sadhana kitchen to prepare a delicious meal that honours your own ancestral heritage. Even if you think that food item is not the most healthy one, because it is part of your ancestry it will be part of your healing. For example, my grandmother used to make big batches of apple strudel, rolling the filo pastry out by hand. This is a skill I would love to master!

♥ Remember the golden chain of teachers before you and behind you and the spiritual lineage of which you are a part. You are not alone in your struggles.

♥ Lie down in a comfortable place and visualise a beautiful place in nature such as a forest or the ocean. Try to 'feel' into as much of this experience as you can. What are the sounds, sensations and fragrances? Even better, lie down in a forest or at the beach and do the same.

♥ If you are struggling with a particular person, situation or problem, enquire into what your gut feeling is about what you should do. Honour your intuition.

♥ Animals and plants can arrive at the perfect moment as powerful guides and helpers. This could be in the form of vibrational medicine, visualisations or visits from wild animals. Start seeing every grain of sand in the natural world as a potential teacher. Are you drawn to a particular crystal or healing herb at this time? This type of awareness is part of shamanic healing culture and helps to awaken

deep memory of the embedded healing codes held within
the timeless universe.

'Everything in the universe is constantly changing, and yet, there are
fundamental rules about how the universe operates which are true
across all time and space. There is a pure ultimate reality that is solid.
In addition to this, there is a kernel of experience that flows through
from one life to another. This is the atman [a Christian might call
it the soul]. Gaining enlightenment means understanding the true
clockwork that makes the universe work. Any person who achieves
Enlightenment understands the true karmic consequences of any
action.' – *Translation from teachings of Dolpopa, Tibetan Buddhist
monk from the 1300s*

## Dharma: your unique life path

In his brilliant book *The Great Work of Your Life*, author Stephen Cope reminds
us of the teachings in the Bhagavad Gita – that the most important service
we can all offer to the world is to authentically uncover and then passionately
follow our dharma in this lifetime. He says: 'In order to have a fulfilling life
you must discover the deep purpose hidden at the very core of yourself. [This
is] the process of unlocking the unique possibility harboured within every
human soul.' Dharma is different for every human being. Sometimes our
dharma unfolds in unexpected ways (I never imagined myself as the mother

of four boys!) and other times more predictably (spiritual longing has been in my heart since childhood).

In our current culture, uncovering our dharma can be challenging because we have so many choices. I'm not suggesting we go back to an age where dharma was set (or locked into a system of social hierarchy such as existed in Victorian England or the caste system in India), but at the other end of this spectrum in which we now live (in the industrialised parts of the world at least) is a seeming sea of endless possibilities. Part of our challenge is finding our calling and then sticking to it.

Art and creativity are so incredibly important for all of humanity. One of the first things military dictatorships and totalitarian regimes remove from society in order to elicit control over the masses is art; books are burned and paintings are destroyed. This is because art inspires us to ask questions, to delve deeper and to look beyond, to break down the walls of separation and to truly see each other – to see each other and to come to know that we are the same.

At a lecture I attended a few years ago a senior Buddhist monk was being asked questions from the audience about spiritual life and Buddhism in general. One audience member asked the monk if he felt we should be giving donations to charity on a regular basis and, if so, which charities specifically we should donate too. The monk's answer surprised me and has stayed with me until this day.

Some people are very skilled at making money and material success; others are skilled at meditation and the spiritual life; others make art and help us to truly open our eyes. All are valid, but according to this wise monk the most valid are the artists – because they are the ones who help us to literally change our minds. The monk suggested that if members of the audience for his lecture had spare money to give, rather than donating to charity they could consider buying art from local artists and supporting writers, musicians and artists in their local area both financially and practically. I found this a liberating and refreshing idea, a total reframing of the plight of the starving artist.

A friend of mine is a successful opera singer. Chatting to her one day she mentioned that she sometimes feels she should be doing more with her life in terms of contributing to the happiness and well-being of others in need. She thought she should be using her time and energy to raise money for charities or campaigning for the environment, something solid and concrete that makes a contribution to the world. I told her about the monk and the talk he gave, and reminded her that her work as a singer put her firmly in the category of artist. Her job is one that makes a huge contribution to the world, through opening people's hearts and minds with her voice. The Bhagavad Gita reminds us time and time again that it is our duty in this lifetime to follow the path of our own unique gifts and talents. We don't get to necessarily choose those talents, but we most certainly should put them to good use when we work out what they are. Part of living a spiritually fulfilled life is to figure out what your unique creative contribution to the world can be – however humble.

In India, wandering sadhus who do the work of meditation and spiritual endeavour are revered members of society. It is an honour to provide food for a sadhu and a privilege to encounter one of these homeless nomads. The work of meditation and spiritual accomplishment is given reverence and respect in Indian culture. Can you imagine the same phenomenon here in our contemporary culture? Sadhus beg for food and live in the wild; they are unconventional and live on the fringes of mainstream society. I'm pretty sure they would not be revered and supported in our culture as they are in Asia. We just don't have the same lens for judgement of what makes a meaningful life and for what makes a contribution to society.

The worst violation of your own spirit is to fail your dharma by doing nothing because you are afraid to fail. What you do doesn't have to be perfect. The Bhagavad Gita tells us that it is better to live your own dharma imperfectly than take on the dharma of another (this includes your parents). I have always had enormous gratitude to my mother for encouraging me to be and do anything good and true I dreamt of, and I hope I can give this gift to my kids.

> *'Ring the bells that still can ring*
> *Forget your perfect offering*
> *There's a crack in everything*
> *That is how the light gets in.'* – Leonard Cohen

At the beginning of this book I wrote about self-confidence and what it means to be truly self-confident. True self-confidence comes from a connection to God and a knowing of the value of your life and the opportunities it offers. We are the blessed ones; we have riches beyond belief, food, shelter, education. To waste this opportunity to be of service is a deep violation of our dharma. Part of this project of aligning with the Divine in order to become lighter and more self-confident is to shatter our own internal glass ceilings, the limitations we place upon ourselves. As we actively work to dissolve our own lack of self-confidence, a dissolving of whatever it is that's holding us back in life occurs. We become elevated and remember as Leonard Cohen so beautifully captured it that we are perfectly imperfect just as we are. In this remembering, there is an unlocking of power; our intuition wakes up (because we finally start listening to it) and our inner compass (dharma) starts to guide us more clearly. This is a process, a constant shedding and letting go, but it begins with lifting our own veils and putting an end to blaming others.

Many people struggle with the feeling that they don't know what their true life path is. This is especially true in our culture where we suffer from having almost too many choices; it's overwhelming. Patanjali gives some very interesting and surprising insight into how we might discover the reason we were born. In the Yoga Sutras, Patanjali says that those who are non-violent will experience compassion. Those who are honest will experience the truth. Those who do not steal will experience abundance, and those of us who are not sexually manipulative will experience good health. And what of those who are not greedy? They will discover why they were born. It seems rather incongruous that greedlessness would lead to an uncovering of dharma, but when we dig a little deeper it becomes apparent why. When you let go of coveting material items you let go of fear. We hold on to stuff because we fear it will be taken from us or that without it we will experience a lack; for example, hunger, a loss of identity or a loss of prestige in how others view us. When we let go of that fear we become absolutely liberated to be who we truly are free of the trappings of material life and the burdens of having to 'achieve' status.

> 'Just by being you, and being unafraid you can be an example to others.' – *Arjuna, Bhagavad Gita*

People who practise yoga are interested in alignment. When we come up into a handstand we're interested in how our shoulders align above our wrists, how our hips align above our shoulders and how our knees align above our hips. This stacking of the joints or more mobile elements of the structure of the handstand allows good alignment which is another way of saying that the structure becomes stable.

When architects draw plans for a high building they will look at the points of weakness and reinforce these structurally; they will design for good alignment in the building so that it is strong. But even structures as solid and immovable as a skyscraper need to be able to move in the wind; they need some flexibility. It's this skilfully designed alignment in the building that allows for the stability and flexibility needed to keep the building standing in high winds or extreme weather. So it is with our handstand or our *tadasana* (mountain pose). We look for alignment, for a sense of steadiness. The building blocks of our posture need to stack neatly and purposefully one upon the other so we can stand on our hands or even steadily on our own two feet on the yoga mat and in life.

Recently I saw an old and frail lady walking down the street. She was very hunched over and stooped. Her posture gave her whole being a resigned air of depression. She was shuffling and sad in her body, and the vibration surrounding her felt shuffling and sad. Young or old, our bodies are mirrors for our mental states, and when we get on the yoga mat we have the chance to realign back into the best version of who we are.

Because of my young family I don't have a huge amount of time for yoga asana practice in my life, and sometimes people ask me what I do when I don't have time to do much on the mat. What I do in terms of the names of the poses varies, but what I do every single day is to re-align. That is, I remind myself of Arjuna's magical teaching; I remind myself of who I am and what my jobs are during this precious lifetime I have been given. I try to hold my head up high and walk with ease. Sometimes I stoop, but yoga helps me to never get too stuck in that way of being.

'We can only become the medicine by becoming ourselves. We can only be happy and a force for good in the world in such chaotic times by becoming ourselves.' – *Amber Magnolia*

# CHAPTER 6

# Subtle energy

*Mapping your energy body and working with the elements*

'For centuries, if not millennia, Eastern medicine systems have held that the human body has two main components. There is the physical self of bones, blood, muscles, nerves and hormones. And there is the subtle body that moves spiritual energy – prana in Sanskrit – through river like pathways called nadis. Instead of a single heartlike pump, the subtle body has seven spinning vortexes called chakras that keep the energy moving through the system. Ultimately energy moves through the body and out through the crown of the head to the divine. When it's healthy energy flows freely and prana moves smoothly along from one chakra to another. But many things can go wrong along the way. When one chakra stops spinning, a channel can get blocked or the entire system can get out of alignment.'

– *Scott Carney*, A Death on Diamond Mountain

## Subtle anatomy

'Just as there exists in writing a literal truth and a poetic truth, there also exists in a human being a literal anatomy and a poetic anatomy. One, you can see and one, you cannot. One is made of bones and teeth and flesh; the other is made of energy and memory and faith. But they are both equally true.'

– *Elizabeth Gilbert*

Recently a friend recommended I check out an art exhibition in my local area. The work on display featured landscapes of Australian sacred sites and areas of natural beauty, of which Australia is blessed with many. On one side of the exhibition were the Western artists' interpretations of particular areas: beautiful depictions of trees and flowers, sunsets, flora and fauna. On the other side of the exhibition were Aboriginal and Indigenous works representing the exact same locations as the Western artists, which showed the same landscapes in very different ways. Waterholes were highlighted, as were dwellings where people lived; food sources and animals were also featured. The paintings were almost like very beautiful maps or guides to the area: totally different in focus from the classic colonial landscape interpretations.

My friend and I chatted about the exhibition and she described that looking at these pieces of art – works which were of exactly the same subject yet so compelling in their differences – made her feel as if the two groups of artists were divided by a glass wall. She described feeling as if each group were pressed up against the glass straining almost to pass through the barrier and see the world through the eyes of another, but the cultural, historical and ancestral backgrounds of each meant that the lenses through which the world is seen were vastly different and largely impenetrable by the other group. It takes a certain kind of magic and a very special kind of artist to be able to transmute through glass walls, but it is possible. This is one of the goals of good art: to help us see the world through another's eyes.

We know that the goal of yoga is to know and feel in our very core the experience of oneness of being. Of course, oneness of being as a phenomenon exists at all times outside of our ability to perceive it. We know that we are all intrinsically linked, we are all one and a part of the web of life – the matrix; we are all in this together. But we forget, because we have been conditioned to see ourselves as separate and we have been born into this container of flesh and blood and bones that we feel is ours and separate to someone else. To know oneness of being is to experience the dissolving of this sense of separation. Some people call it enlightenment, or liberation. When artists help us to dissolve the glass walls that separate us and prevent us from seeing the world as others do they help us move closer to oneness of being. If we could see the world through the eyes of a child or a cow or a mountain or the earth herself – even if only for a moment – we would behave in radically different ways.

Just as there are metaphorical glass walls that divide us and prevent us from seeing the world through the eyes of another, so there are glass walls within us that divide one part of us from another. The wall between mind and body is an obvious one. There is also a wall that separates the subtle world from the gross material plane.

Some techniques such as meditation and yoga, when used in the right way and under the guidance of a skilful teacher, can help us to break down the glass walls so that we can experience the subtle realms more freely. We've all had that experience; for most of us the moment of falling asleep, of waking up and of orgasm are all times when the wall breaks down, even if only for a few seconds, and the veils between gross and subtle are thin. These times when we are connected to our subtle bodies are also often times when we are most receptive to our own creativity. When we connect to the subtle realm the material (gross) realm drops into the background and our creative spirits are given an opportunity to flourish.

## Reading maps of the body

'We think this physical body we have is very robust and solid and the connection to it is strong but it's as simple as the string holding the mala beads together. It could snap at any minute and we'd be into the realms of rebirth to the next "bead". It's actually a very tentative connection we have to this body. The subtle body and the buddhi with it are far greater. Far more solid and magnificent.'

– *Maya Tiwari*

Not so long ago, in the time before mobile phones and satellite navigation, if you wanted to go somewhere new you had to read a map and figure out how to get there. You might look at the map and contemplate which highway would be most efficient, or whether to take the slower but more scenic route. We also use maps to explain and understand the human body. Doctors and medical practitioners make maps of our muscles and bones and body systems in an attempt to gain deeper understanding of the way our incredible human form works. These medical maps can be very useful, but they are limited.

Depending on what we want to know we may consult different types of maps; for example, if you are going hiking you may consult a map that shows contour lines so you can anticipate how many hills you will be climbing. If you're covering the same territory via aeroplane, the contours of the Earth's surface matter less and a flight path map would be more useful. In the same way, the anatomy and physiology maps of the body only tell part of the story.

The saints and sages of ancient times saw maps in their meditations and visions that are guides for those of us interested in metaphysical exploration of the human form. Meta means 'bigger than', so these maps go beyond the physical into the subtle realm. They are metaphysical because they go beyond that which we can explain with science or specifically physics alone.

'There are many rivers inside a human body, thousands of miles of blood vessels. That is just the physical level. On the level of the prana body there is similar intricacy … and invitation to listen to the life flow within. It is always there, rushing like a river, a whisper. Once in a while you may hear it while meditating, especially in the early hours of the morning before dawn.'
– *Lorin Roche*, The Radiance Sutras

The ancient yogis gave us a framework of signposts (chakras) and pathways (nadis) and described the movements of energy (prana) in their carefully constructed and intricately detailed maps. True understanding of these maps may lead to yogic siddhis or magical powers previously considered impossible. The maps show us the way to new uncharted territories within our very own body vehicle.

Seeing is believing, and the experience becomes the evidence or the proof we might need if feeling cynical. That is why when I wrote about God at the beginning of this book I suggested that even if you don't believe in a higher power you might want to try prayer, because the proof is in the experience. What we can usually see is limited to our sensory ability to perceive. A dog perceives the same item such as a pen differently from a human being. The dog sees a chew toy; we see an implement for writing. We all perceive the same things differently according to preference and cultural conditioning, among other factors. How do we open our sense gates more widely and shift our perceptions? One way is to practise yoga with an open heart and mind and a spirit of playful experimentation.

Through the practices of yoga, we can explore the maps in our own bodies; they are available to us! When we shift our perception, we start to see ourselves and the world in more magical ways and deeper experience becomes available to us.

'There are planets, solar systems and galaxies, if one speaks of them there is no limit, no end. There are worlds upon worlds of creation.' – *Guru Nanak, from ancient Sikh scripture and Kundalini Yoga lineage*

I once saw a beautiful picture online from the European Space Agency that looked like lots of colourful bubbles floating through a pink sky. The image came from the Hubble telescope viewing what are technically described as (I am not kidding here) cosmic space bubbles. Cosmic space bubbles actually do exist and they are beautiful! I thought I was the only one living in a cosmic space bubble, but apparently we're surrounded by them. If you feel a bit shut down about the possibility of energy and prana and the mysteries of your own body, think for a moment about all that we don't know out there in space. It's a vast, unknown universe and it starts inside your very being. In remembering the vastness and the unknown and celebrating the mystery of the universe we can also celebrate the mystery of our own incarnation and life. Reflecting on this makes me feel tiny but somehow still important, like a honey bee or an ant.

'You cannot be with the wild ones if you fear the rumbling of the ground, the roar of a cascading river, the startling clap of thunder in the sky.' – *Alison Nappi*

## Elemental beings and our symbiotic relations with nature

As well as being a way of looking at our bodies, energy-based paradigms offer a way of looking at the Earth. Contemporary schools of thought such as permaculture and knowledge of biorhythms and moon phases in human bodies and in nature (used for growing crops, as one example) are actually reflections of teachings we can see in the Bhagavad Gita. In Chapter 3, Krishna gives Arjuna some information about how humanity interacts with the energy of the Earth and other beings that dwell on the Earth. Krishna talks about the *devas*, which are sometimes translated as 'demi-gods' but which we can think of as benevolent energetic presences who will help us if we nourish the Earth and all upon it. Some folklore traditions have different names for these entities such as fairies or angels. The Bhagavad Gita tells us that if we cherish and nourish these entities by supporting their habitat (Mother Earth) we will be cherished and nourished in return.

This may sound far-fetched but, really, it's just a simple teaching in energetic exchange – it's an equation. What you put out there will come back to you; space is curved. I avoid putting lots of photographs of my children on the internet because I don't like the idea they are available for anyone to look at and interact with. An image of my child is an energetic imprint of him, and it is sacred to me and the preservation of the purity of my son's energetic or subtle body. In exactly the same way, if we put pictures of our ancestors in our homes and honour them or if we put a picture of our teachers, guru and God on our altar and perform sacred ceremony for them we directly impact the energetic exchange of both our relationship with those holy beings and even the images themselves. The images take on the vibrations of the subject and come to life, which is how energy works in our bodies in our interactions with the Earth and in the whole cosmos.

Aboriginal wisdom also gives some guidance on the elemental forces and energies around us. There are special, more magical times of the day, for example, starting at pre-dawn and ending with sunset followed by the silence of the night. Seasonal cycles have names that give clues as to their energetic qualities, such as 'time of fire', 'cooling time of renewal', 'time of cold' and 'warming time of renewal'. The yearly calendar doesn't rely on dates in the months or even solstices, but on key events in the environment. Specific plants flowering and fruiting and noticeable quirks in animals' behaviour that only occur at certain times of the year mark the passing of time, not a regimented calendar. This is an intuitive way of living deeply connected to the land and the energy of it as not separate from us or the passing of time.

Thousands of years of living within, observing and understanding the rich Earth herself has led to a deep knowing beyond science. For Aboriginal people the devas manifest in the forms of spirit entities living on and within the land. Elemental beings were in the caves, mountains and red sand of the desert, and Indigenous peoples lived harmoniously with them before colonialisation. This is the true application of the Gita's teaching of 'thus nourishing one another, there will reign general prosperity for all' (Bhagavad Gita translation: Srila Prabhupada, Chapter 3, verse 11). In these times of global warming and environmental degradation, we might ask ourselves what is left of this knowledge and relationship.

If you find this dialogue around energy and the unseen spirit world a little out there and confronting, just keep in mind there is room for both hard cold facts and intuitive resonant knowing to sit side by side. In fact, as quantum physics evolves as a subject it is morphing more and more into a challenging set of mixed messages that encompass way more magic than most cynical scientists feel at home with. A naturopath friend of mine told me recently she likes to think of herself as 'clinically based and magically minded'. I love that: one foot firmly in the practical earth the other in the sparkle of the ethers.

'The human body is a great blessing. A form through which to explore energy. Even if it has not been your habit through your life so far, I recommend that you learn to think positively about your body.'

– *Ina May Gaskin*

## Working with the elements

*'Earth my body,*
*Water my blood,*
*Air my breath,*
*Fire my spirit.'* – traditional pagan goddess chant

According to ayurveda our subtle bodies, just like our physical bodies, are impacted by the seasonal cycles and the five elements. Each one of us has a unique constitutional type that is set at the time of birth. This constitutional type can be thought of as a mixture of the four elements within our bodies and personality types. Some people are very grounded, earthy and soulful; others are more flighty, airy and emotional. Most of us are a mix but with a predominance of one or two elemental tendencies, which usually start to show up in childhood. In ayurveda your unique constitutional type is called your dosha and it describes the tendency you will have to go out of balance.

There are three doshas: pitta is fire, vata is air and kapha is earth combined with water. For example, a fire/pitta person will be especially exacerbated on a hot summer day, whereas an air/vata person will feel especially out of balance in very windy weather. The following chart gives some indications of the ways in which the elements connect to the ayurvedic doshas, the seasons and our five senses. Exploring and widening the capacity of our senses allows us to feel and experience the many facets of the self and awaken the journey to self-knowing more deeply. When we get to know our unique constitutional type we can learn how to balance it by working with the elements. To go back to our pitta type, who is burning up in the summer sun, jumping in the ocean will be the perfect antidote.

| Element | Direction (southern hemisphere) | Ayurvedic dosha | Associated stage of life | Qualities | Season | Five senses |
|---|---|---|---|---|---|---|
| Water | East | Kapha (with earth) | Maiden (0-25) | flourishing growth blossoming | Spring (rebirth) | Taste |
| Fire | North | Pitta | Mother (25-50) | energetic daytime active social | Summer (celebration) | Sight |
| Air | West | Vata | Maga (50-70) | dry movement transition | Autumn (harvest) | Touch |
| Earth | South | Kapha (with water) | Crone (70 to death) | inward slow wisdom | Winter (rest) | Fragrance |
| Space | All directions | Sound is the element for space. In the Jivamukti Yoga tradition we have a teaching that 'sound is God'. This comes from the Hatha Yoga Pradipika, and suggests that through sound vibration (for example, chanting mantra) we can reach higher states of consciousness. We might say sound is the most sacred of our five senses and space the most subtle of the elements. | | | | |

In ayurveda, and interestingly Aboriginal wisdom, there are six seasons. But for the ease of understanding I've simplified it to the four seasons we are most familiar with plus space. Let's explore a little more how we can use the elements in combinations with our five senses as part of our daily sadhana practices. It will be most powerful if you focus on a particular element and sense during the season to which it relates, but if you feel a particular element is out of balance the practices can be helpful at any time. If you are new to ayurveda do not worry too much about the stages of life; when you first start working with the elements in this way it's easier to focus on your own individual tendencies (dosha) rather than other factors such as age, which are more subtle in their impact.

## Elemental practices

### Earth

**Physical practice:** take off your shoes and socks and stand tall in tadasana (mountain pose). Visualise a mountain you know of or have visited and really try to embody the feeling and vibration of that mountain. Feel steady and connected to the Earth, particularly through the soles of your feet. A mountain never questions its presence on the Earth or its relationship to the elements around it and the weather passing over it. The mountain just 'is' and is confident in its mountain qualities. In other words, the mountain knows its dharma is to be a mountain. In the yoga asana of mountain pose we can embody this same confidence and steadiness. To go deeper into the Earth vibration, visualise the richest, deepest compost you've ever seen or touched, the type of fertile compost that keen gardeners get really excited about. Now imagine the bowl of your pelvis inside your body is filled with that soil. Feel it densely packed, stable and solid. If you have any hyper-mobility in your body, especially around your sacrum or lower back, imagine that soil being packed around the mobile areas, creating stability and a feeling of security. This practice is especially helpful in post-natal recovery, where vata dosha is usually very high and there is often a feeling of inner emptiness as well as overly mobile joints.

**Food practice:** the Earth element connects to fragrance. Use the smells of your cooking to enliven your spirit: baking bread, roasting coffee or the wonderful aroma of freshly ground spices frying in oil.

### Fire

Fire is the element of action and burning through that which is not of service to us or the higher good. Fire is an essential element in social activism and relates to the middle phase of our lives when we are most active and engaged in worldly activities.

**Physical practice:** stand tall with your hands on your hips and your knees slightly bent. Begin to swing your arms around your body as you rotate a little from side to side; you can go as fast or as slow as you like. Your breath should be steady, and as you do the movement visualise a fire burning in your belly. This is the fire of digestion (called *agni* in Sanskrit). The arms move like a helicopter's blades. If you get really into it you can extend the movement into a fire dance, allowing your arms to swing around freely and embodying the fire in your belly that so many traditions acknowledge. In Traditional Chinese Medicine it is your 'hara' and in yogic tradition the location of your manipura chakra. Another option for increasing your fire energy is to wear red underpants.

**Food practice:** notice the colour and texture of spices, fruits and vegetables as you prepare them. Create a beautiful setting for your meals using colourful fabric napkins and beautiful flowers as a centrepiece.

## Air

The element of vata tends to over-dominate in our culture. Sometimes vata is praised as holding a capacity to multitask, but what this means in reality is often distraction and overwhelming. Multitasking can quickly become an excuse for poor focus and a lack of attention span, both of which can manifest in vata imbalance. The use of devices such as smart phones and other technologies often exacerbate this type of vata imbalance, the antidote to which is to get grounded. Gentle deep breathing can help us to manage the air element in our bodies skilfully. Because the air element relates to our sense of touch, self-massage (or receiving a massage from someone else) can be a great health management tool for air-type people. Massaging coconut or sesame oil (not toasted) into your body before a shower or bath is a good way of adopting this practice into your daily routines and oiling the body is effective for vatas, especially if you focus on rubbing oil into the bony areas such as joints and cartilage.

**Physical practice:** stand tall with your legs hip width apart and feet firmly planted into the earth. Extend your arms above your head with your fingers interlaced and only the index fingers extended straight up. Take a deep inhale. As you exhale, soften your knees and swing your arms between your legs; the image is one of a woodchopper cutting wood with a big axe. As you do this movement take a long strong exhale out of your mouth and make a loud sighing noise. This is the 'air' part of the practice – the forced sighing exhale. Repeat for between five to ten rounds. This is a great stress-relief practice that is also grounding. It is a good practice if you've been sitting at a desk or driving a car for a long period of time, or if you are very frustrated with someone or something.

**Food practice:** the air element is connected to the sense of touch. When cooking experience the pleasures of touch in everyday food preparation. Use your fingers to mix ingredients, and measure them out (one handful is an 'anjali' in Sanskrit). Feel shiny beans running through your fingers and rice trickling through as you rinse it.

## Water

Environmentalists are telling us that water is the new oil, meaning that the need for clean water will always be there but the supply on planet Earth is dwindling because of pollution and abuse of our water systems. There are many ways we can take action to protect the water sources, such as avoiding mass-produced factory goods (particularly clothing, where dyes and processes are huge polluters of waterways), not eating fish or switching to sustainable fisheries and switching to natural cleaning agents and bathing products. Energetically, the water element relates in our bodies to good-quality rest, something most of us could do with more of.

**Physical practice:** jump in the ocean, a river or a lake as often as possible. If you can't access a natural body of water, a shower or long luxurious bath is a good second option.

**Food practice:** the water element manifests as taste, which in ayurveda is represented by the balance of six specific tastes in your food: sweet, sour, salty, pungent, bitter and astringent. The balancing of these six tastes creates delicious food and has many healing qualities.

## Space

Although space relates to the sense of sound, manifest in this element is the idea of silence and stillness. The chakra or energy centre located at the heart in our bodies is named in Sanskrit *anahata*. This means 'unstruck sound', and pertains to a subtle teaching that says when a certain state of absorption is reached in meditation, sounds spontaneously arise within our consciousness that are not arising from an outside source. Scriptures describe these sounds as being like buzzing bees, drums and even the movement of clouds through the sky. Meditating on these sounds is powerful and facilitates their spontaneous arising during silence. Perhaps this is one reason why in shamanic practices the drum journey is so powerful as a technique for allowing insight to unfold.

**Physical practice:** listen to the sounds of nature, animals and insects around you. Chant holy mantras and prayers. Surround yourself with sacred sound vibrations.

**Food practice:** hear the sounds when preparing your food such as the pounding of spices and grains or the crisp sharp sound of cutting vegetables.

# CHAPTER 7

# Home

*Spiritual activism begins with each of us in our daily lives
and our homes*

'Each one of us has the power to shift global consciousness
into the mind of peace. Peace is about learning to transcend
disharmony, disorder, disease and despair by reaching for that
inner flame the irrevocable, incorruptible light that restores
harmonic conditions in our cultures, communities and in ourselves.'

*– Maya Tiwari*

## Be a good example

One of the most popular slokas from the ancient Indian scripture, the
Bhagavad Gita suggests that, for progress on a spiritual path, we should let
go of attachment to outcomes and of the need for acknowledgement for our
actions. The teaching is that we will gain more from our efforts if they are
offered unconditionally and anonymously.

'As the ignorant perform their duties with attachment to
results, similarly the learned may also act, but without
attachment, for the sake of leading people on the right path.'

*– Bhagavad Gita translation: Srila Prabhupada, Chapter 3, verse 25*

This verse is well known and often quoted, however, the sloka that immediately follows and which is much less famous is also of great value in my opinion and deserves deeper contemplation. The Gita goes on to suggest that the
way in which we will see unconditional service and selfless action manifest
and bearing fruit is if we endeavour in all that we do to be a good example to
others. We might interpret this by remembering that others usually do as we

do, not as we say (particularly our family members and children). Ultimately, we act in life as an example to the Divine. Another way of thinking about this is that we step up to doing our very best in all situations and context even if we think no one else is watching. We do not act only out of accountability or social impact; we act with love in service of God's love.

Not so long ago one of my children was struggling a little with reading at school. I started to research methods for learning to read and investigated ways in which I could support him. I was astounded to find in one Swedish scientifically conducted study what it is that is most helpful in supporting young people with reading. The study found that when young children are surrounded by adults who read regularly and who have a love of books this will have *more* impact on their own reading development than time spent with an adult one on one actually teaching a child to read! Being around a culture of reading has a greater effect than being taught to read. This amazed me and it illustrates perfectly the point being made in the Bhagavad Gita:

> **'By continuously performing selfless actions the wise person influences others in all they do.'** – *Bhagavad Gita translation: Swami Satchidananda, Chapter 3, sloka 26*

We are also reminded earlier on in this chapter in the Gita that it is pointless to try to 'disturb the mind of an unwise person' by nagging them or pointing out the error in their ways. Srila Prabhupada says it like this: 'Therefore a realized soul in Krishna consciousness should not disturb others in their activities or understanding, but he should act by showing how the results of all work can be dedicated to the service of Krishna.' *Be an example and don't*

*preach* is the overall message here. If we want others to be grateful to us or to look up to us because of our efforts or wisdom then we are automatically negating the fruits of our hard work – we are no longer engaged in karma yoga or selfless service but rather in doing things well for our own benefit or desire for reward. Swami Satchidananda says in the Living Gita: 'Actions of service should be done perfectly, even neater and tidier because they are offerings. Whatever you do for your own sake can be ordinary, but when you do it for others, you're doing it for God.'

As a parent and a yoga teacher, this teaching has been of enormous value to me. I have practised over time truly attempting to live what I teach and what I ask for from my family. If I want my children to spend less time staring at screens I need to put my own phone away. If I want them to eat less meat I need to be a living example of a healthy and joyful vegetarian. So it goes. I do not do these things because I expect a particular outcome; I do them in loving service (and because they enrich my life), and with a 'swaha' I let go of outcome and offer up my efforts.

This is such a liberating and calming way to live and creates harmony in situations that would otherwise be tense and stuck with judgement, expectation and disappointment. It also helps if I remember that ultimately my efforts alone do not determine the outcome of my actions: 'Things get done only with the cooperation of energies completely outside our control … but persons who think themselves independent in their actions make the mistake of taking credit (or blame) for everything they do.' – Joshua Green, *Gita Wisdom*

Part of this teaching is also that we could encourage those less adept than ourselves to practise, which goes back to the example of my son and his reading. I don't show off how great I am at reading or make him feel bad that he can't read; I just support him in his efforts, acknowledge that it's a process and celebrate his development.

'The learned know better than to discourage the less learned from acting. Rather, they offer encouragement, knowing people are [sometimes] confused.' – *Bhagavad Gita translation: Joshua Green, Chapter 3, sloka 28*

Many yoga teachers (and parents) would do well to remember this lesson: the joy of the journey and of effort rather than end results or comparison with others. A great deal of what is wrong with our developed world school systems, and our society as a whole, has its roots in competition and numbers-based records of achievement. There is much to be gained in learning for the love and passion of the subject, for its intrinsic value.

'I believe the new activism in this time is fighting for and freeing your mind, body, and emotions from the hypnotic media haze, denatured nutritional vitality suppression, and the general culturally accepted commotionality and subsequent fatigue we call "living a life".' – *Guru Jagat*

## Sadhana krama

There is a sequence through which we move if we practise sadhana with diligence that takes us deeper into our relationship with the Divine and amplifies our intuition and spiritual practices to the places where magic can arise. B.K.S. Iyengar calls this the 'sadhana krama'. Krama relates to a sequence of moments. You may know the word krama in the context of physical asana sequences – a strict flow of movement connected to the breath is known as vinyasa krama, which pertains to a sequence of moments linked through breath and movement. Sadhana krama also links a sequence of moments (your life!) to conscious spiritual practice. If you find your life unfolding as a sequence of moments grounded in conscious spiritual practice, Iyengar states you will start to move through the layers of yourself (koshas) from the more gross and mundane to the more subtle and sublime. Through sadhana krama you will be elevated to spiritual insight. For Iyengar the practice of sadhana is a conscious spiritual practice, in sequence.

## The koshas

Let's take a deeper look at this sequence that Iyengar and many other yoga masters have explained with the map of the koshas.

The koshas or 'sheaths' are layers or levels at which we can experience the Divine in our lives. They are our human material bodies and our spirit soul in combination. We tend to think of ourselves as having one body only, but according to yogic teachings your body has five distinct parts. Material existence embodies the first three and the last two are transcendental; that is, beyond time and space.

The first kosha is *annamaya* kosha, which is the realisation of the Divine based on food otherwise known as your human body. This precious body is yours for one lifetime only, and the scriptures tell us that to take birth in human form is an enormous blessing because it gives us the opportunity to evolve spiritually. We have such mixed attitudes to food in our culture and all of them represent our relationship to this primal kosha or layer of our being – our 'food body'. Taken literally, this kosha is the very embodiment of 'you are what you eat'. When we waste food or indulge excessively we are squandering the beautiful potential of that relationship. When we say grace before eating or prepare food as an offering of love and devotion we embrace the highest potential of this layer. Food can harm or heal the health of our bodies, the animals and the planet herself. If you eat the flesh of another being you feed your food body with the fear and suffering that animal experienced before death. If you eat food low in prana or life force like junk food you deplete the food body. If you eat organic fruits, vegies and grains you will thrive – it's a very simple equation! Food is a foundation level of existence. We need food to live, and the provision of that food is a blessing that we often take for granted. We can heal the anamaya kosha with a healthy plant-based diet, with yoga asana and with kriyas or cleansing practices.

The next level of potential for knowing the Divine using your human form is through breath and energy. Life in the physical body is vulnerable. We celebrate our health and vitality by means of breathing, and if we are really fortunate we go deeper through practices like yoga asana and pranayama to actively work with this incredible potential. This is *pranamaya* kosha, the subtle energy sheath or layer.

Third and still dwelling in the material plane is *manomaya* kosha (some-times known as *jnanamaya* kosha). Manomaya relates to the idea of thought processes; jnana means 'knowledge or wisdom'. Whichever translation you choose this kosha relates to our precious faculty of attention – our ability to think and how we process our thoughts. This fluctuation of the mind can distract or disturb us or take us closer to spiritual liberation depending on how we harness it. The yogic scriptures warn us not to waste this mental faculty on material gain or manipulation, but rather to focus it on spiritual consciousness. We could also place ahimsa (non-violence) at the forefront of our consciousness as part of elevating manomaya kosha.

For many people who experience depression and other mental health challenges this layer is where healing needs to take place, as evaluating our own thought patterns and habits can help to heal them. One method for this is meditation in which we practise watching the mind think; in Sanskrit this is called the sakshi, which means 'witness'. This is enormously helpful in understanding that we are not our thoughts. The very fact that we are able to witness ourselves and notice changing thoughts as they transiently pass through means there is something beyond the thoughts that is able to watch. At the same time you are able to witness yourself thinking, which is a very hopeful message for those struggling with anxious or depressed thinking cycles. This kosha can be healed in a few ways. In modern psychology, we might take a therapeutic or cognitive approach psychotherapeutically. This can be helpful, but yogic teachings would say it is a limited approach.

To get deeper we can use three powerful practices. The first is the practice of ethical constraints, such as Patanjali's yama and niyama. When we live in accord with our deepest values (for example, living with compassion, not lying, not stealing, not degrading others, not being greedy), our thinking has less opportunity to get muddied and dark. Patanjali says that of all the ethical considerations, ahimsa or non-violence (compassion) is the most powerful in transforming chitta vritti (whirling mental patterns). So this practice of ethics in action can help enormously with our mental states. The second method for healing manomaya kosha is karma yoga or the yoga of selfless service. Working hard for the benefit of others, helping wherever we can, has enormous benefit for ourselves as well as the recipient of our good deeds. The final and by far the most powerful way to heal manomaya kosha is through the practice of bhakti or devotion. When we dedicate our lives to something or someone greater than our small selves or ego we become unbound by the limitations of material experiences and even our own mental states. We realise either in a flash of knowing or in a slow and steady dawning over time that we were meant for much more.

The treasures in spiritual evolution come when we let go of the fluctuating and impermanent material koshas or layers and connect to the higher two. We step beyond the mundane and into the sublime 'eternal spiritual identity different from the body and mind' (Devamrita Swami). In this way we become more interested in knowing God than in gaining a promotion at work.

> 'The Bhagavad Gita invited us to drink at the fountain
> of sacred activism. To be in the world but not of the world.'
> *– Devamrita Swami*

In practice, this means that as yogis we nourish our bodies with the best plant-based food and prasad (food prepared in sadhana) that we are able to. We remain connected to our breath and the energy cycles within our bodies and we acknowledge the power of the mind and our thoughts. At the same time, we realise we are not all these things alone; there are some hidden jewels beyond the body and the mind.

In the fourth stage, the vijnanamaya kosha, we experience the soul or spirit beyond name and form; we experience some part of ourselves that is not our mind or our body. This can happen for some sports people when they get into the zone and even during the experience of deep pain in the physical body when we might start to disassociate. For flickering moments the realisation arises that we are more. It is also possible to access knowledge of vijnanamaya kosha through the use of mind-altering intoxicants such as recreational drugs. These methods usually have many side effects, including ultimately pulling the user further away from spiritual progress of any kind. In my experience the safest, most effective and easily replicated (with practise) way to access this experience is in meditation or through other spiritual practices such as chanting.

The study of sacred scriptures and Sanskrit language can also have a profound impact on vijnanamaya kosha. Whereas the lower three koshas are purified and healed mostly though effort, when we work with the higher two an element of grace is involved. This fourth kosha is most readily accessed through our feelings and elevated emotional states. We cannot think our way into it; we can't achieve this level of awareness-expansion by will and effort alone. There is some magic involved, which scripture can help us to access by, among other benefits, reminding us that many have worked hard on this path before us (we are not alone) and that we can benefit from their efforts through the lineages that pass this sacred knowledge down.

In the fifth and final stage, anandamaya kosha, we realise our connection to universal consciousness – our connection to God or, rather, God in us. This is sometimes known as oneness of being, because we realise we are all part of the web of life and not separate from it. Sometimes this is called the bliss body or bliss layer, because we cannot help but feel deep relief in the knowing of what is truly important. This body is like a candle burning within our hearts; it might be covered by much dust or many layers, but it is alight all the same. We feel the results of our good deeds through this kosha and we need it to transform into uncovering the spiritual beings we really are. It is also helpful to remember that every human being contains this core of potential goodness within them, even those who we don't like or who we see committing negative actions. The potential for transformation is always there.

'Without the essential ingredient of Bhakti, which means "devotion or love for God" sadhana will not yield anything interesting or magical.'

– *Sharon Gannon*

## Beginning at home

The word 'home' has in its centre the vibrational syllable 'om'. How can we move from the more basic survival of eating and breathing into higher realms of spiritual awareness in our own lives? The good news is that even through the simple (and necessary to life) acts of eating and breathing we have the opportunity to get closer to consciousness. However, if we're not careful we will get stuck in those more mundane mechanisms and forget to aspire to more. How can we move through the koshas or layers of ourselves into connection and the blissfulness of knowing our true spiritual nature? One powerful way I know of to remedy this is through what Buddhists call mindfulness but what I like to think of as ceremony. Through simple practices of ritual and awareness as basic as lighting a candle, setting up a sacred space at home or burning some incense or sage you will start to see your home as a temple.

Each month at Jivamukti Yoga we are given a short essay ('The Focus of the Month') as an inspiration from which to teach. The topics range enormously but always cover yogic teachings. One of my absolute favourite focus of the month essays came from my teacher Sharon Gannon and was titled 'Three Steps'; it was about cooking, cleaning and gardening (January 2011). It tells the story of Sharon's very first spiritual teacher, who gave her the instruction that she could get closer to God through these mundane but necessary activities. Sharon was repelled by these teachings – she wanted something more transcendental and sublime – but in time she came to embrace their value. She started to see cooking as an opportunity to practise ahimsa through serving delicious food to her friends and family and inspiring them to consider a vegan diet. Many years later she has now written a vegan cookbook. She realised that through gardening (even something as simple as herbs in pots on the windowsill) she could connect her food to its source and the magical alchemy behind all of life.

Perhaps one of the reasons this teaching was so powerful for me when I read it was that I was spending a lot of time looking after young children at that time (and still now!) and it just resonated so deeply that my daily life was my opportunity to go further in my spiritual life. The two were not separate; they were the same. As Sharon said: 'Without mastering the seemingly ordinary basics of living, no spiritual maturity, much less real spiritual evolution, is possible. One has to first grasp the magic in the ordinary before the extraordinary dawns, and once it does the everyday is the same as it was before – only sweeter.' This describes exactly how the teaching of the koshas can be seen as a method for moving from the gross to the subtle or the mundane to the elevated.

## Ceremony

'Craft a life you are proud to live in.
Don't be deduced by boredom or cynicism.'

*– Ana Forrest*

Ceremony in your daily life means to set a guiding intent, or as yoga teacher and ceremonial matriarch Ana Forrest says to 'craft your life'. You may feel that life is coming at you. Through ceremony and intention setting you will feel more and more that you are shaping your life – perhaps not the events that unfold, but certainly your perceptions of and responses to them. You will start to shift into feeling that your surroundings are sacred space in which you can create a ceremonial experience. Ceremony is a way of waking up each day and bringing your best self forward.

## How to use ceremony in your daily life

♥ Bless yourself and your space with smoke (from incense or burning sage or bay). Go through the gates of initiation in this simple way: walk forward in each day with awareness. I also use my practice of japa meditation and mantra recitation as a method for this morning cleansing and setting my attention in the right way for the day ahead.

♥ Prepare for difficult conversations with ceremony by getting into your higher self. A yoga teacher friend of mine was recently interviewed for a radio show during which she spoke about her preparation, saying that she wanted to speak from her heart and be a channel for the teachings. She did this by taking a bath with rose oil in it to ritualistically prepare herself. She also followed an ayurvedic protocol of eating something bitter before the interview, because bitter foods are said to keep the mind sharp.

♥ If you are a yoga teacher, bring ceremony into your classes. Ana Forrrest starts each class with a smoke blessing. If this is not possible for you, perhaps you can use a singing bowl, the chant of 'om' or the setting of intention as ceremony for creating sacred space.

- ♥ It is important that ceremony doesn't become routined or perfunctory. The power is in the focus and attention you bring.

- ♥ Ceremony around food can involve offering some food on your altar or sacred space at home or saying a blessing before eating your meal.

- ♥ Use ceremony for manifestation: ask your soul, your higher two koshas, 'what do you want?' The answers will almost always involve getting closer to Spirit. Set your intentions and envision your highest self, then take that intention into the actions of your daily life.

- ♥ Use ceremony to problem solve: go into ceremony to breathe into contemplation. Quest for solutions and find tools to help you with your struggle. When something goes wrong, find the intuitive thread. Where did you ignore your gut along the line? Your gut and intuitive nature is a resource when it comes to problem solving.

- ♥ Light a candle or incense stick as a way of taking a sacred pause in your day. As you do this, check in with your breath and scan your awareness through your body, releasing any areas of tension you are unconsciously holding, particularly around the neck and shoulders.

Through ceremony and the practices of bringing mindfulness and a sense of sacred ritual into your daily life you will find that your dharma is awakened more deeply. When you become very deliberate and aware of your daily habits, rhythm and flow your actions become aligned with your values. Actions aligned with your deepest values represent you living in your true dharma or life's calling. This is the potential power of ceremony, which can add resonance to how we relate to others and to the quality and texture of our decision making. In truth, these practices transform the quality of our whole being.

Part of making space for ritual and ceremony in your life is to also make space to daydream. Ceremony may help you with making art and connecting to your innate sense of creativity. I find it very difficult to sit down and write if I haven't cleared my physical and energetic space first. I tidy up, clean a bit, burn some palo santo or sage and take a few rounds of mantra recitation – only then do I feel ready to work creatively. This process of setting up the energy doesn't have to take long (and shouldn't be an excuse for procrastination!), but it will make you more efficient and effective in all your work.

'All artists connect the dots differently. We all start off with all these live, fresh ingredients that are recognizable from the reality of our experiences (a heartbreak, a finger, a parent, an eyeball, a glass of wine) and we throw them in the Art Blender. All art no matter what shape it is, has to come from somewhere. We can only connect the dots that we can collect.'

*– Amanda Palmer*

Through ceremony and setting up your space, you can choose where you focus your energy and what you collect and transmit. Observe how you think: what are the stories that arise in quieter, sacred moments? How does your creativity flourish? What quality are the ingredients you are pouring into your creativity smoothie?

## Notes on parenting

As a mother of four children I have put great thought into creating a home that is a sacred space, not only for my own spiritual development and sanctuary but also for my family. Yogi Bhajan often used the word 'cosy' when describing the yogic family home and this is an image close to my heart. Please do not think this means my home is an example of tranquillity and peace all the time; it is loud and messy and full on and I often raise my voice (I'm working on doing so less, mostly unsuccessfully). I do have a few very clear and non-negotiable systems in place that maintain our home as an area of sanctuary and solace, for not only my family but for all who visit and spend time with us. I've been very inspired by the teachings of Rudolf Steiner, a great visionary in the field of education. To the wonderful Steiner-based teachers and mentors who have influenced me, I offer enormous gratitude. So here are some practices specifically for creating a calm and sacred home for children:

♥ Creating good habits around sleep will serve the whole family. All of the five koshas get refreshed in sleep. Burn some lavender oil, take a bath, eliminate all light from the bedroom and turn off all screens for a good night's sleep. Attempting to go to bed around the same time every night will also help.

♥ It is good to have firm boundaries where children are concerned. You don't always need to explain your position as a parent. One of the best Steiner teachers I know, who has been a parenting mentor to me, suggests that taking your authority in a kind and loving way is our role as parents. Your job is to hold the space, sometimes fiercely, which may mean acting counter culture and sometimes being disliked by your children. Limit screen time and insist on good food habits: this is part of your dharma and will to parent. Many parents get caught up in wanting to make their children happy at the cost of decisions for higher good. This is particularly true of the need to buy your children lots of things they think they need and want. If you can, give your children your time and attention rather than stuff.

♥ Both Steiner education and Traditional Chinese Medicine speak of the importance of physical warmth for children. In winter, place a warm hot water bottle or wheat pack under your child's feet. Computers and screens have the effect of energetically cooling and encourage disengagement, so try to keep them out of the bedroom, especially at bed time. Warmth is the flame of life and love for children.

♥ Steiner also taught the importance of living your own will as parents in order to model fullness, rather than emptiness. I interpret this as living your dharma, which is important for two reasons as a parent: first, because it will encourage your children to do the same, and second, because then you won't project your unfulfilled dreams and ambitions onto your children. This will leave their psyches free to discover their own dharma.

♥ In order to nourish the annamaya kosha (the food body) in children there are two very important factors apart from obviously what they actually eat. The first is sitting down as a family and eating together. I want to emphasise this to you, as it is so important. I know it's messy, noisy and not that relaxing, but I can honestly tell you based on years of experience of having a sit-down-together-as-a-whole-family dinner every night that it is of great, great value. Most of the families I know give their children dinner early and then the parents eat separately later. I understand the reasons why, but I want to encourage you not to do that. The conversations (arguments even) that happen over dinner are important, along with the valuable modelling of eating nicely together. We all eat the same food (no special kid's food) and we all eat together at least once a day. We set the table with napkins and candles and everyone helps. The television is off and there are no phones or toys at the table. I don't usually spoon feed my younger children; as soon as they are old enough to pick up a spoon or fork they feed themselves. I am raising four boys who are wonderful eaters with great table manners and a healthy and grateful attitude to food in this way. The second important factor here is in involving children in preparing and cooking food. We talk about what we will eat. There are always a range of healthy options to choose from on the table and all the children are involved in different ways in creating our meals, from growing to serving.

## Enlightenment in our times

The English word 'enlightenment' pertains to the historical time after the Renaissance. The Enlightenment period in Europe was a time of great technological, artistic and social revolution. The intellect flourished, and logic and rationality replaced superstition (which was one of the reasons many wise women and healers were attacked at this time and labelled negatively as witches).

In Sanskrit the word 'bodhi' relates to enlightenment in terms of an intrinsic knowledge of the world. The focus is on changing oneself rather than the world around us. In addition to enlightenment on behalf of oneself, the Buddhist bodhisattva vow emphasises the commitment to work towards the enlightenment of all beings.

I am highlighting this linguistic and conceptual history in order to demonstrate that the idea of enlightenment means different things to different people and has a very different history in Western culture than it does in the East. Perhaps that is why it's not a term we immediately relate to for the most part within our culture. Ideas such as happiness or joy seem more tangible than the abstract nature of enlightenment, so what can enlightenment mean for us? How can we access the potential of this lofty goal?

One element of enlightenment is in the walls of division dissolving away. We experience less and less our separation from the world and others and feel more and more connected. There is an indigenous tribe in Mexico that describes the enlightenment experience as being one of completion; that is, we become complete and experience a feeling of returning to source. Imagine the benefits even a glimmer of this sense of connection could have if our world leaders, famous people of influence and powerful corporate decision makers experienced it.

One key to coming closer to the experience of oneness in our own lives lies in the company we keep: 'The bhakti tradition teaches us to maintain balance in our relationships and how we use our time. Spending time with like-minded friends for example allows us to wrap ourselves in spiritual armour. This protects us from becoming frustrated or bewildered by negativity. It empowers us to be respectful, kind and faithful to our values. We reach for love, truth and spiritual joy.' (Radhanath Swami)

In order to experience God or these glimpses of enlightenment for ourselves we might also have to get quiet, to step outside of the noise of contemporary culture that pulls our attention in many unhelpful directions. Author

Emily P. Freeman describes this quietness so beautifully: 'The delicate grass of the kingdom is being formed in you. Don't trample all over the seeds. Instead, sit down and see what God is growing.' Freeman is wise enough to know that this quietness is counter culture and a challenge for many of us. It is difficult to embrace the mystery and the abstract when we are so conditioned to only relating to that which we can easily see and engage with. Freeman says: 'Most of the time I'd rather stomp on the sprouts of growth than stand on tiptoe to see the faint outline of hope. I don't want to live in the invisible kingdom. I want to be in charge and in control.'

So one of the deepest lessons we can learn on our spiritual journey is to inhale 'let' and exhale 'go' and stand on the edge of hope, not bombarding ourselves with bulldozers of control that come from fear of the unknown.

Enlightenment in a moment can be as simple as coming into relationship with your breath.

'Behind the sun and the moon and the brook and the rustling leaves is silence, and it is that silence that the human is drawn toward. We call this mindfulness, the basis of sadhana. Silence is what we yearn for. It is what feeds us.' – *Maya Tiwari*

The nourishment of silence and quiet time alone is available to us regardless of our status, financial situation, education or background. It is perhaps the antidote to the confusion of our modern world. It is in this silence and stillness, perhaps in the practice of meditation or japa recitation or perhaps in simply sitting and being quiet for a few precious moments, that true healing can take place. Also, the heart-opening capacity within us can unfold to incorporate more than an egocentric view of the world. In his book *The Unsettling of America,* Wendell Berry beautifully sums up a holistic approach to healing:

> [Our bodies] are not distinct from the bodies of plants and animals, with which we are involved in the cycles of feeding and the intricate companionships of ecological systems and of the spirit. They are not distinct from the earth, the sun and moon, and the other heavenly bodies. It is therefore absurd to approach the subject of health piecemeal with a departmentalized band of specialists. A medical doctor uninterested in nutrition, in agriculture, in the wholesomeness of mind and spirit is as absurd as a farmer who is uninterested in health. Our fragmentation of this subject cannot be our cure, because it is our disease.

When we relate to our own bodies as part of the cosmic body we start to experience our own healing as part of a greater healing. When we practise tend and befriend as a response to stress rather than fight or flight we reduce the stress hormones running around our nervous systems, and healing takes place rather than an escalation of anxiety and animosity. In this way peace begins in our own body and our homes and expands out into our communities and greater world. If our own energy lines (prana nadis) are not clogged and dampened down by stress, we can be of greater service in the world.

It is my own personal experience over many years that the practice of meditation and japa has enabled me to access this stillness and the resultant connection to source more than any other techniques. Meditation is a cleaning out of your mental garbage. You wouldn't leave your house full of trash, so why your mind? Meditation is challenging because it is the antithesis of how we live now, especially in a mobile phone culture. We are becoming screen addicts, and as a result have to fill every moment with stimulation or risk the boredom of time with nothing happening. But it is in the nothing happening moments that we can notice what is really happening. This teaching from an Aboriginal elder explains beautifully:

> To fully understand or become intimate with something is to know its story. So, you could go to your sitting place and really look at, for example a lemon, and think about how to understand its story. It's good to practise on fruits and to become intimate with their stories – you'll feel safe because they are unlikely to trigger your opponents. Everything has a story and everything has a teaching. When you have become confident with fruit you can go to your sitting place and start to give yourself time to really look at different emotions. First you need to let go of all the garbage. (Minmia, *Under the Quandong Tree*)

Sitting in stillness teaches us how to focus. We find in the Bhagavad Gita that Arjuna is the best warrior because of his ability of focus. He has mastered the art of doing the outer work (activism) with an eye to the inner work (sadhana).

In a book written over twenty years ago, Marianne Williamson understood this concept perfectly:

> For the traditionally minded feminism in politics means more women voting and more public policy supporting us. Certainly, these things are important. But feminism should have a much more expanded meaning. It is not just the role of women in society but also the role of genuinely feminine, yin facets of consciousness that must emerge reborn. In the century now dawning,

spirituality, visionary consciousness, and the ability to build and mend human relationships will be more important for the fate and safety of this nation than our capacity to forcefully subdue an enemy. (Marianne Williamson, *The Healing of America*)

Here on planet Earth we can still see the light from dead stars. This is the perfect metaphor for hope. We have yet to see the light from newborn stars: What a wonderful and mystifying concept! I hope the practices of sadhana in your everyday life will help you to engage with all that fills you with hope. In this hopeful magic of bhakti, we can build communities that reach out into the world and cultivate hopeful situations. Through your sadhana practices you can find and stay connected deeply to a place of Spirit and meaning and be an active participant in this life you have been gifted. It is with great love that all is possible.

# Glossary

*Abhyanga*: oil massage traditional in ayurveda.

*Agni*: digestive fire in the stomach.

*Ahamkara*: ego; the sense of self we need in life in order to learn and grow.

*Ahimsa*: non-violence.

*Anjali*: a handful Traditional way of measuring food; for example, one anjali of rice.

*Arjuna*: protagonist of the sacred scripture Bhagavad Gita, a spiritual warrior who has a crisis of faith on the battlefield.

*Asana*: physical postures of yoga; the literal translation is 'seat'.

*Ashtanga Yoga* (Patanjali Yoga Sutra system): eight-step system for attaining enlightenment that includes yoga postures, breathing practices and meditation among other techniques.

*Ashtanga Yoga* (Pattabis Jois system): vinyasa (breath linked with movement) yoga asana system that works progressively through set sequences, starting with the primary series.

*Asmita*: ego as bound into self-identity. A hindrance to spiritual growth.

*Ayurveda*: wisdom of life. Health and wellness protocols that together form the traditional Indian healing system.

*Bhagavad Gita*: the Lord's Song, in which Krishna speaks to Arjuna; an ancient yogic scripture.

*Bhakti*: the act of devotional, loving service.

*Buddhi*: capacity of the intellectual mind to discriminate and analyse; the greater mind.

*Chakra*: a spinning vortex located in the subtle body that keeps energy moving through the system.

*Chitta vritti*: fluctuations and chatter in the mind.

*Dharma*: your true calling in this lifetime; the skills and gifts you have to offer into the world.

*Dinacharya*: daily routines for health according to ayurveda.

*Dosha*: your unique constitutional type according to Ayurveda; your personal tendency toward imbalance.

*Ganesh*: Hindu deity with an elephant's head; represents the removal of obstacles.

*Hanuman*: Hindu deity in the form of a monkey; represents strength and devotion.

*Ida nadi*: energy channel that runs around the spine and ends at the left nostril.

*Japa*: chanting using mala beads and the recitation of a mantra in repetition.

*Jivamukti*: liberated while living. Jivamukti Yoga is a style of yoga founded by Sharon Gannon and David Life in New York City in the 1980s.

*Jnana mudra*: a hand configuration that channels specific energy where the index finger (representative of ego) is curled under the thumb (representative of God).

*Kapalabhati*: literal translation 'shining skull'. A breathing practice that cleanses and brightens the mind using a repetitive forced exhale.

*Kapha*: ayurvedic dosha or constitutional type represented by earth and water.

*Karma*: literal translation 'action'. The teachings of karma are complex and offer insight into the impact of what we think, say and do. Karma teachings are closely connected to teachings around reincarnation.

*Kirtan*: devotional chanting of mantra, usually in a group context with musical accompaniment in a call and response style.

*Kosha*: layer or level of the 'self'; the physical human body and spirit soul in combination. There are five koshas.

*Krama*: sequence, specific order.

*Krishna*: The Supreme Lord;  God.

*Kriya*: internal purification practice such as breathing, or cleansing practices.

*Mala*: beads used for chanting practice.

*Mantra*: literal translation 'to transcend the mind'. Sanskrit phrase or verse used in chanting.

*Medha*: the intellect illuminated by love; associated with female intelligence.

*Patanjali*: yogic saint who wrote a scripture known as the Yoga Sutras over 2,000 years ago.

*Pingala nadi*: energy channel that runs around the spine and ends at the right nostril.

*Pitta*: ayurvedic dosha or constitutional type represented by fire.

*Prana*: life force or energy.

*Prana nadis*: nadi means 'river'; prana means 'life force'. The channels or rivers in the body through which life force flows; somewhat like meridians in Traditional Chinese Medicine.

*Pranayama*: breathing practices; control of prana or energy in the body.

*Prasad*: food prepared in the spirit of conscious spiritual practice and as an offering to the Divine.

*Puja*: devotional ritual such as burning incense or offering flowers to an altar.

*Sadhana*: conscious spiritual practice; to act in the world and remain deeply connected to Spirit.

*Sadhu*: spiritual practitioners who live a nomadic life outside of normal society.

*Sakshi*: inner witness; ability to observe ourselves in thought.

*Samskara*: impressions created by actions (karmas) we perform; subtle impressions or residues held within the body/mind complex as a result of our choices.

*Sankulpa*: resolve; prayer; intention; spiritual promise or commitment.

*Sanskrit*: ancient Indian language of poetry and philosophy.

*Sattvic*: pure and light. One of the three gunas or 'states in nature'; often refers to food.

*Seva*: selfless service, such as volunteering to cook for those who are hungry as an act of spiritual offering.

*Shakti*: Divine feminine; force of creation; powerful.

*Shiva*: Divine masculine; Hindu deity.

*Siddhi*: magical power arising through yogic practice; for example, the ability to levitate.

*Sloka*: verse of scripture.

*Sutra*: literal translation 'stitch'. Verse or stitch of text suitable for memorising.

*Tanmatra*: subtle element. Unadulterated core vibration and energetic configuration; usually relates to food, for example, a seed that is not genetically modified has its tanmatra intact.

*Upanishads*: ancient yogic scriptures. Literal translation is 'to sit at the feet of [the teacher]'.

*Vata*: ayurvedic dosha or constitutional type represented by air.

*Yoga*: to 'yoke' or absorb into the Divine; to move closer to God.

*Yoga nidra*: yogic sleep; guided deep relaxation.

# Bibliography/ acknowledgements

Dasi, Visakha (ourspiritualjourney.com): Five Years, Eleven Months and a Lifetime of Unexpected Love.

Devamrita Swami (howicame.com): Searching for Vedic India; Hiding in Unnatural Happiness.

Forrest, Ana (forestyoga.com): Fierce Medicine.

Gannon, Sharon (jivamuktiyoga.com), Cats and Dogs are People Too; Art of Yoga (with David Life); Jivamukti Yoga (with David Life); Yoga and Vegetarianism; Yoga Assists (with David Life); Simple Recipes for Joy; The Magic Ten and Beyond.

Gilbert, Elizabeth (elizabethgilbert.com): Big Magic; Eat, Pray, Love.

Guru Jagat (ramayogainstitute.com): Invincible Living.

Hardwicke Collings, Jane (www.janehardwickecollings.com).

Horton, Lauren/Astrid (www.singingbirdyoga.com).

Levin, Jordanna (www.jordannalevin.com).

Lister, Lisa (lisalister.com): Witch.

Magnolia, Amber (mythicmedicine.love).

Manorma (sanskritstudies.org).

Matthews, Shaun (ayurvedichealing.com.au).

Minmia (minmia.com.au): Under the Quandong Tree.

Nappi, Alison (rebellesociety.com).

Norberg-Hodge, Helena (localfutures.org): Ancient Futures.

Palmer, Amanda (amandapalmer.net): The Art of Asking.

Prince, Milla (thewomanwhomarriedabear.com).

Rabbath, Rima (soukofrima.com).

Radhanath Swami (radhanathswami.com): The Journey Within; The Journey Home.

Roach, Geshe Michael (geshemichaelroach.com): The Diamond Cutter; How Yoga Works.

Roache, Lorin (lorinroache.com): The Radiance Sutras.

Roy, Suzanna Arhundati: The God of Small Things; The End of Imagination.

Safran Foer, Jonathan: Eating Animals.

Tiwari, Maya (wiseearth.com): Women's Power to Heal; The Path of Practice: A woman's book of ayurveda healing.

Williamson, Marianne (marianne.com): A Woman's Worth.

Katie Manitsas is an advanced-level Jivamukti Yoga teacher and a Wise Earth Ayurveda master teacher. She is also qualified in Kundalini Yoga and as a doula (childbirth support person), and holds the highest possible accreditations with both Yoga Alliance and Yoga Australia. She has been teaching yoga for over 20 years.

Katie's passion is in yogic philosophy and the seasonal practices of sadhana, bringing devotion and a sense of the sacred to everyday life, as well as compassion for animals and a deep reverence for nature. Katie is a published author of several books, including *The Yoga of Birth*. She is the mother of four young boys and lives with her loud and busy family in Sydney's Inner West.

Katie can be contacted at katie@katiemanitsas.com.au and details of her workshops and events can be found at www.KatieManitsas.com.au.

*Other books in the series ...*

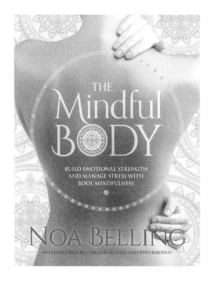

# The Mindful Body
## Noa Belling

ISBN 978-1-925682-18-2, 216 pages, paperback book, 230 x 179mm

How does your mind live in your body? How can body awareness help you change your mind and experience of life? Successful author and practicing psychotherapist Noa Belling offers a practical, personal way to use your body as a direct path to mindfulness and mindful living.

By waking up to how we hold life experience in our bodies, we have the power and choice to improve physical, mental and emotional health, promote vitality, build emotional resilience and generally improve quality of life.

Supported with psychological and neuroscientific studies, this book provides you with many opportunities to practice body mindfulness to experience your physical being as an empowering and intelligent resource.

Available online at www.rockpoolpublishing.com.au or
all good bookstores.